FIFTY SEO IDEAS:
Free Tips, Secrets, and Ideas for Search Engine Optimization

2013 EDITION

by Jason McDonald, Ph.D.
© 2012, JM InternetGroup
www.jm-seo.org
Tel. +1-510-713-2150

CONTENTS

0

INTRODUCTION

Welcome to *Fifty SEO Ideas! SEO*, of course, stands for *Search Engine Optimization*, the art and science of getting your company to the top of Google's free results, for free, using free SEO tips, tools, and techniques. While SEO certainly sounds wonderful, getting your company to the top of Google can seem overwhelming. Why do some companies show up on page one of Google, while others are buried pages deep? What are the technical tips and tricks that propel a product or service to the top of the search engines? And why do so many people talk about SEO yet so few seem to actually know anything concrete about how to get it done?

Fifty SEO Ideas aims to make SEO easy by giving you a playbook of simple, practical SEO to-do's. Great cooks like Julia Child taught cooking one recipe at a time, while great coaches like Vince Lombardi taught football one play at a time. *Fifty SEO Ideas* helps you understand SEO one idea at a time. That said, *Fifty SEO Ideas* is not a step-by-step guide to SEO! It is an *ideabook*: a book of ideas, in no particular order. It is meant to spur your own thinking, for you to read a suggestion and say to yourself, "Yes, that's for me!" or "No, that doesn't really apply to my needs." For a systematic step-by-step system of SEO, please refer to my *SEO Fitness Workbook* on Amazon or my online classes at JM-SEO.org. *Fifty SEO Ideas* is meant to get your juices flowing, and to break SEO down into easy-to-understand, easy-to-implement doable ideas.

Let's get started!

To Do List:

>> Meet the Author and Understand How this Workbook Works

>> Bookmark Links for Help and More Information

>> Browse the Table of Contents

>> Read the Copyright and Disclaimer

>> Meet the Author and Understand How This Workbook Works

My name is Jason McDonald. I have been active on the Internet since 1994 and teaching SEO, AdWords, and Social Media since 2009 — online, in San Francisco, at Stanford University Continuing Studies, at workshops, and in corporate trainings. More than 1,300 people have taken my paid trainings; over 14,000 have taken my free webinars. I love figuring out how things work, and I love teaching others! SEO is an endeavor that I understand, and I want to empower you to understand it as well. You can find out more about me at http://www.jasonmcdonald.org.

Fifty SEO Ideas works as follows. Each SEO tip has three bullets explaining it at the "executive summary" level. There is then a paragraph explaining the tip in more detail, plus a to-do list of step-by-step instructions. You are asked to rate the relevance of each tip to your own business or organization and to grade your performance to date. Finally, where appropriate, I give pointers to free

Internet resources where you can learn more or implement the tip in greater detail. *Fifty SEO Ideas* is an ideabook, so please flip through it like you might flip through a cookbook or playbook. Use the ones you like, and ignore the ones you don't — and hopefully find a few ideas that you just hadn't thought of.

More Free SEO Tips
Want more tips? Write a **review** on Amazon about the book (good, bad or ugly), send me an email (info@jm-seo.org), and I will give you a bonus PDF of **ten** additional *SEO Ideas* as my way of saying thanks. If you have a tip or suggestion, please email me directly. If I use your tip in the next edition, I'll give you that edition — free!

Acknowledgements
No man is an island, and no book is truly the production of just one person. I would like to thank my wife, Noelle Decambra, for her research skills, patience, and editing skills. Diana Ecker refined my grammar, edited the final book, and taught me that it is now officially one space (and not two) at the end of each sentence. Gloria McNabb, as always, helped not just with research but with her cheerful disposition in the topsy-turvy world of SEO. Most of all, I would like to thank my students — at Stanford, in San Francisco, and online — who teach me every day through their questions and motivate me every day through their enthusiasm.

▶▶ Bookmark Links for Help and More Information

Here are important links for help and more information

- **Book Resources Online** — for a PDF version of this book, including all web links and resources, go to http://www.jm-seo.org/promo and enter the password "**ideas**."

- **YouTube Videos** — "how to" videos on YouTube at http://www.youtube.com/jmgrp that give step-by-step instructions on important tactics like setting up effective landing pages or syndicating free press releases.

- The **JM Internet Group** website at http://www.jm-seo.org. Don't miss the blog, the SEO tutorial, and the SEO tips section. The company also provides free webinars and "on demand" tutorials on SEO, AdWords, and Social Media marketing — just click on the "free" icon.

Questions? Email info@jm-seo.org. As someone who loves to teach, I work really hard for my students and readers, so I strongly encourage you to email me with any questions. Don't hesitate!
- *Jason McDonald, Ph.D.*

▶▶ Read the Copyright and Disclaimer

KEYWORD DISCOVERY

FREE KEYWORD TOOLS HELP IDENTIFY AND TARGET SEO KEYWORDS.

CREATE STRONG SEO CONTENT!

- Keywords drive Google and SEO, yet most organizations lack a structured list.
- High-volume, high-value keywords return the best ROI in search.
- Keywords are useful for SEO, AdWords, and even Social Media.

DESCRIPTION: Keywords drive Google and SEO! The user types in a keyword search to start the process, and Google interprets the relationship between these keywords and the websites in its database to produce the resulting ranked list of websites. Having a systematic understanding of your keywords is arguably the most important step in successful SEO. Yet many companies do not know their keywords, lack a systematic keyword worksheet, and do not measure their rank across keywords over time. Moreover, the real return on investment occurs at the intersection of high-volume keywords with high-value keywords, yet few understand the relationship between keyword volume and value. Fortunately, free keyword tools can help you with keyword discovery, keyword volume, and keyword value.

BEST FOR: All organizations.

DO THIS: As needed.

TIME TO COMPLETE: A few hours or less.

HOW IMPORTANT IS THIS IS TO YOUR BUSINESS?

< **Not Important – Neutral – Very Important** >
☐   ☐☐☐   ☐

WHAT GRADE DO YOU GIVE YOUR COMPANY ON THIS TASK?

☐ **Not Relevant | Grade: < F –D – C – B – A >**

TO-DO'S

- Brainstorm your keywords to get started.
- Use free keyword tools to build a "universe" of target keywords.
- Use the Google keyword tool to drill down and identify volume and value.
- Build a structured keyword worksheet.
- Measure your keyword success in Google Analytics.

The person assigned to do this is: _____.

Deadline to complete: _____, 201_.

INTERNET RESOURCES

Google Keyword Tool

If you are setting up a pay-per-click advertising campaign and/or working on your own SEO strategy, this free tool from Google is very helpful. Enter a keyword and Google will show you the number of recent searches for that keyword as well as related keywords, with which you can determine interesting adjacent keywords for your SEO efforts. https://adwords.google.com/select/KeywordToolExternal

WordPot

This is a fantastic keyword discovery tool. Enter a keyword and get a list of phrases and synonyms. One of our favorites for the all-important keyword discovery phase of SEO. http://www.wordpot.com/

Google Suggest and Related Searches

These tools are embedded in Google itself. Type a target keyword phrase into Google, and pay attention to the suggested keywords in the pull-down menu. This is called "Google Suggest." Many of these are great SEO keyword phrases to target. Next, type your keyword phrase in, hit enter, and then on the menu on the left, click on "Show search tools." You will see an option called "Related searches." Click there and you will find a great list of search phrases related to the one you just entered. http://www.google.com/

KeywordSpy

KeywordSpy currently operates in the United States, the United Kingdom, Australia and Canada. With this keyword tool and keyword software, you can perform advanced keyword research and keyword tracking to study what your competitors have been advertising in their AdWords campaigns and other PPC campaigns. You can get complete in-depth analysis, stats, budget, affiliates & ad copies of your competitors. http://www.keywordspy.com/

2

SEO KEYWORDS

IDENTIFY YOUR TOP SEO KEYWORDS IN GOOGLE ANALYTICS.

CREATE STRONG SEO CONTENT!

- Keyword research is incredibly important to SEO.
- You can use Google Analytics to see what keywords people are searching for.
- If you advertise on AdWords, this information is available in great detail.

DESCRIPTION: Keywords are the heart of SEO. Using the free Google Keyword Tool, you can guesstimate the volume and value of potential keywords. But what happens once you get your website working? Use Google Analytics to drill down into the actual keywords that people are using to get to your site. Even though Google has reduced the sharing of this information, it still gives you a good idea of what keywords are actually performing for you. If you are advertising on AdWords, you can drill down to even more nuanced information on the ACTUAL keywords people use to get to your website. Then brainstorm opportunities! (Don't forget, however, that Analytics shows ONLY the keywords that you are succeeding at. If you have no Google rank for a keyword, you won't get any traffic).

BEST FOR: All organizations.

DO THIS: Monthly.

TIME TO COMPLETE: A few hours or less.

HOW IMPORTANT IS THIS IS TO YOUR BUSINESS?

    < Not Important – Neutral – Very Important >
       ☐   ☐☐☐   ☐

WHAT GRADE DO YOU GIVE YOUR COMPANY ON THIS TASK?

    ☐ **Not Relevant | Grade: < F –D – C – B – A >**

TO-DO'S

- Define a marketing question you want answered, such as Texas customers vs. NY customers.
- Login to Google Analytics, click on Advanced Segments, and new custom segment.
- Select your parameters in the menus provided, such as medium = organic for organic, SEO traffic.
- Don't forget to use the Google Analytics "help" function if you do not understand the vocabulary!
- Save your Advanced Segment and use it as a window into a specific segment of your web traffic.

The person assigned to do this is: _____.

Deadline to complete: _____, 201_.

INTERNET RESOURCES

Google Analytics

Google Analytics is the enterprise-class web analytics solution that gives you rich insights into your website traffic and marketing effectiveness. Powerful, flexible and easy-to-use features now let you see and analyze your traffic data in an entirely new way. With Google Analytics, you're more prepared to write better-targeted ads, strengthen your marketing initiatives and create higher converting websites.
http://www.google.com/analytics/

AUTHORSHIP ON GOOGLE

SET UP A GOOGLE+ PERSONAL PAGE AND CREATE AUTHORSHIP.

CREATE STRONG SEO CONTENT!

- Google+ helps with SEO, and authorship enables your picture to show on Google.
- Setting up a business Google+ is different from claiming an individual Google+.
- Once set up, cross-reference your Google+ to your site via authorship.

DESCRIPTION: Google+ is the new social media kid on the block, and he has a very powerful daddy: Google. By setting up a personal Google+ account, you can build a community of followers around you. And by enabling "authorship," you can get your picture to show on Google searches for your relevant keywords. Note that "authorship" currently only works for individuals, not companies, so you need to identify a company spokesperson (business owner, CEO) to post content on Google+, encourage followers, and cross-reference to your website content, including blog posts.

BEST FOR: All organizations.

DO THIS: As often as possible.

TIME TO COMPLETE: A few hours or less.

HOW IMPORTANT IS THIS IS TO YOUR BUSINESS?

> **< Not Important – Neutral – Very Important >**
> ☐ ☐☐☐ ☐

WHAT GRADE DO YOU GIVE YOUR COMPANY ON THIS TASK?

☐ **Not Relevant | Grade: < F –D – C – B – A >**

TO-DO'S

- Set up an individual Google+ account.
- Follow the steps for authorship (see YouTube video below).
- Once enabled, check authorship via the Rich Snippets Testing Tool.
- Post frequently, and encourage the growth of a follower community.
- Watch your picture show on Google searches, enabling a "virtuous circle.

The person assigned to do this is: _____.

Deadline to complete: _____, 201_.

INTERNET RESOURCES

Google+

Google+ is the new kid on the social media block. So far, it hasn't succeeded to the extent of Facebook, but it is growing daily. Google is incentivizing companies and individuals to use Google+ by allowing author photos to appear on Google searches, if the user a) has a Google+ profile, b) has sufficient Google+ followers, and c) has implemented the steps to enable authorship/rich snippets. So your first step is to set up a personal Google+ profile for your company spokesperson.
http://plus.google.com/

How to Get Your Picture on Google Search Results (and YouTube Video)

It's called authorship, and it isn't as hard as it is detail-oriented. This tutorial post explains step by step along with a YouTube video the steps you need to take to get your picture to show on a Google search.
http://www.jm-seo.org/seo-tutorial/authorship-rich-snippets.html

Google Rich Snippets Testing Tool

Once you've a) set up your Google+ personal page, and b) correctly enabled rich snippets/ authorship per the above tutorial, you can use Google's Rich Snippets Testing Tool to confirm that it is working correctly.
http://www.google.com/webmasters/tools/richsnippets

Google Authorship - The Official Page

Here is the official page on authorship from Google. It's a little overcomplicated, but they do explain that there are actually two methods of enabling authorship. Choose the one that will be easiest for you: email authentication or rich snippets. (One issue with email authentication is that it increases your spam risk).
http://www.google.com/insidesearch/features/authorship/index.html

LOCAL CITATIONS

CLAIM YOUR LOCAL LISTINGS AND SOLICIT LOCAL CITATIONS.

PROMOTE YOUR COMPANY!

- Citations are references to your website, including your physical address.
- Google uses external citations as verification of your status in local SEO.
- External websites such as Yelp or Citysearch are valuable for SEO.

DESCRIPTION: How does Google know where your business is, and how does it know that this information it has is reliable? If someone searches Google for "San Francisco CPA Firms," how does Google know which businesses are truly in San Francisco, active, and worthy of being on page one of the search results in the coveted "local listings" section? One factor in this answer is the presence of citations. Citations are references on external websites that verify your physical location, especially your address. Make it easy for Google to understand your citations by claiming your local listings and making them consistent in the way that they display your address, city, state, and telephone number. Finally, encourage reviews across local sites to further improve the citation effect.

BEST FOR: Local businesses.

DO THIS: One time.

TIME TO COMPLETE: More than a few hours.

HOW IMPORTANT IS THIS IS TO YOUR BUSINESS?

< **Not Important – Neutral – Very Important** >
☐   ☐☐☐   ☐

WHAT GRADE DO YOU GIVE YOUR COMPANY ON THIS TASK?

☐ **Not Relevant | Grade:** < F –D – C – B – A >

TO-DO'S

- Use Google to identify which local listings matter for your keywords (see below).
- Find your listing on both Google+ Local and other local sites like Yelp or Superpages.
- Make each listing consistent, with the exact same address and phone.
- Encourage reviews across local listings sites to further improve your citation quality.
- Don't forget to identify local bloggers, as local blog SEO can help citations, too!

The person assigned to do this is: _____.

Deadline to complete: _____, 201_.

INTERNET RESOURCES

Google

Use Google to identify OTHER, NON-GOOGLE local listing sites. 1) Go to google.com and enter search keywords that trigger local results (Google+ Local results). 2) Find a competitor who has many reviews. 3) Click on his or her "x Google reviews" link to view the Google+ Local listing. 4) Scroll to the very bottom, where it says"Reviews from around the web." 5) Click on those and you have found other, non-Google sites that do local listings for your keywords. Then claim and optimize your listings on those sites.
http://www.google.com/

Get Listed

This cool tool will check to see if your business is listed and findable on Google Places, Yahoo, Yelp and other local search sites. It is one of the few tools available for cross-checking of local search, and a great one to try.
http://getlisted.org/

Google+ Local (Formerly Google Places)

Google+ Local is the place to find and claim your free local listing from Google. Once you find your listing, you will be prompted to claim it via telephone or postcard verification. Then be sure to beef it up with a keyword-heavy company name and description. Be sure to have one standard format for your business name and address across all local listing sites.
http://www.google.com/places

Google Authorship - The Official Page

Here is the official page on authorship from Google. It's a little overcomplicated, but they do explain that there are actually two methods of enabling authorship. Choose the one that will be easiest for you: email authentication or rich snippets. (One issue with email authentication is that it increases your spam risk).
http://www.google.com/insidesearch/features/authorship/index.html

LINK BAIT

BRAINSTORM "LINK BAIT" OPPORTUNITIES LIKE INFOGRAPHICS OR WIDGETS.

PROMOTE YOUR COMPANY!

- Inbound links matter tremendously to Google and SEO!
- Links can be hard to get, as few people link outward.
- Link bait means novel ideas such as infographics, widgets, etc.

DESCRIPTION: Links matter a great deal to Google, as Google interprets links as "votes" on the Web. If website A has 50 inbound links from other websites, and website B has only 25, then, all other things being equal, website A will outrank website B on Google searches. Like votes in an election, inbound links propel websites to the winning positions. Moreover, the structure of links (keyword-heavy targets in the A HREF tag) and the authority of the linking websites factor into the Google algorithm. One part of an effective link-building strategy is to brainstorm link bait. Link bait refers to useful widgets such as BMI calculators, the real-time price of gold, or even infographics, that other people find so compelling they blog about it, tweet it, and otherwise link back from their website to your website (where the bait resides). So if you can create a "link bait" idea, you get an amazing SEO benefit: a link-building campaign on autopilot, for free!

BEST FOR: All organizations.

DO THIS: As often as possible.

TIME TO COMPLETE: More than a few hours.

HOW IMPORTANT IS THIS IS TO YOUR BUSINESS?

    < Not Important – Neutral – Very Important >
    ☐   ☐☐☐   ☐

WHAT GRADE DO YOU GIVE YOUR COMPANY ON THIS TASK?

    ☐ **Not Relevant | Grade: < F –D – C – B – A >**

TO-DO'S

- Brainstorm "link bait" ideas that you would like to develop.
- Reverse engineer competitors' sites or cool sites to ponder their link-building strategies.
- Choose and build your favorite widget, infographic, or other link bait idea.
- Promote the link bait to your core customers.
- Hopefully start a virtuous viral cycle wherein people continually link to your bait.

The person assigned to do this is: _____.

Deadline to complete: _____, 201_.

INTERNET RESOURCES

Visual.ly
Visualizations are powerful, but they have always required time and hard work to create -- until now. You no longer need expensive software, extensive design skills, or number-crunching ability. Visual.ly is building a tool that will allow everyone to quickly and easily create professional quality designs with their own data. And when you're ready to show your work to the world, publish it on your Visual.ly profile, your own personal showcase. http://visual.ly/

Monex Price of Gold Widgets
This is an example of link bait. Monex is a provider of gold bullion, and the company provides these nifty widgets in HTML format for free on their website. Bloggers, journalists, and others download the code -- and presto, instant link back to Monex. Note the "embedded" ALT attribute to the image and transfer of" link juice": link bait in action. http://www.monex.com/resources/

ReverseMortgage.org - Reverse Mortgage Calculator
Here is another example of link bait in action: a nifty, free reverse mortgage calculator. Journalists, bloggers, and others link back to this tool, thereby subtly promoting Reverse-Mortgage.org to Google as a relevant site for "reverse mortgage." http://www.google.com/places

BBB (Better Business Bureau) Links
Icons like those used by the Better Business Bureau, GoDaddy, W3C consortium and others have a link bait function. Sites link back to them to prove that they are accredited, and thereby pass link juice to the target site. http://bit.ly/QGR944

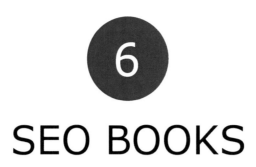

SEO BOOKS

STAY ABREAST OF SEO BOOKS VIA AMAZON.COM SEARCHES.

LEARN SOME TIPS, TRICKS OR SECRETS!

- Books explain SEO in a coherent, logical format.
- Use Amazon to stay abreast of the latest books.
- Many books have websites with free PDFs, tools, and downloads.

DESCRIPTION: The Web is full of blog posts, articles, top ten lists and other content. That's all well and good. However, explaining search engine optimization concepts and practices comprehensively requires a longer format: the book. Many SEO experts publish books explaining their philosophy of how to do SEO, breaking SEO down for you systematically step by step. Amazon makes it easy to preview these books and order your favorites in physical or e-book format. If you like to read, books on SEO are one of the best ways to stay current with what really works.

BEST FOR: All organizations.

DO THIS: Whenever.

TIME TO COMPLETE: Each time, a few hours or less.

HOW IMPORTANT IS THIS IS TO YOUR BUSINESS?

< Not Important – Neutral – Very Important >
☐   ☐☐☐   ☐

WHAT GRADE DO YOU GIVE YOUR COMPANY ON THIS TASK?

☐ **Not Relevant | Grade: < F –D – C – B – A >**

TO-DO'S

- Go to Amazon.com.
- Search for SEO in books.
- Organize by "most recent."
- Preview interesting books, and order the ones you like best.
- Set aside some time to read books on SEO as part of your self-education strategy.

The person assigned to do this is: _____.

Deadline to complete: _____, 201_.

INTERNET RESOURCES

Amazon.com
Amazon.com is the world's largest bookstore, and their search engine makes it easy to search for SEO books. Just go to Amazon and search for "SEO." On the far right, you can sort by publication date. In that way, you can find the newest books coming out on SEO and even pre-order copies. Even if you don't order a book, Google the author's name and "SEO" and you can often find an author or book website with free PDF and tool downloads!
http://visual.ly/

Top Ten Best SEO Books, Ever
Looking for the best SEO books? For small business and marketers, here are my top recommended books on SEO. Some bring you the SEO fish. A few teach you how to SEO fish. I teach Search Engine Optimization online for the JM Internet Group -- just Google "Jason McDonald" to find me. Many times my students ask, "Hey Jason, what are the best books on SEO? What books would be top-rated? What SEO books would you recommend?" So here's my list.
http://www.amazon.com/Top-Best-SEO-Books-Ever/lm/R2ZJ80G4COWMSZ

GOOGLE ALERTS

SET UP GOOGLE EMAIL ALERTS TO MONITOR YOUR KEYWORDS.

MEASURE OR MONITOR YOUR PERFORMANCE!

- Track mentions of your company for free using Google email alerts.
- Google monitors the web, social media like blogs and Google+, and news 24/7.
- Leverage Google Alerts for competitors and keywords, too.

DESCRIPTION: Wouldn't it be fantastic if there were a free service that "clipped" every mention of your company in a blog, a new website, or even a news service, and then faithfully sent you an email alert when that "mention" happened? Guess what? Google Alerts is exactly such a service! Sign up for Google Alerts, input your company name, and Google will happily email you every time your company name appears in a new blog post, new website page, or news mention. Even better, use Google Alerts to monitor your competitors' names or even your industry keywords. For free, Google keeps you abreast of the buzz across the Net on the topics you care about most. In SEO terms, it's a useful way to identify people linking to your content, or even to see when Google actually indexes content on your own blog or website.

BEST FOR: All organizations.

DO THIS: Weekly.

TIME TO COMPLETE: A few hours or less.

HOW IMPORTANT IS THIS IS TO YOUR BUSINESS?

   < Not Important – Neutral – Very Important >
   ☐   ☐☐☐   ☐

WHAT GRADE DO YOU GIVE YOUR COMPANY ON THIS TASK?

   ☐ **Not Relevant | Grade: < F –D – C – B – A >**

TO-DO'S

- Sign up for a free Google Account, such as Gmail.
- Go to the Google Alerts website, or do a keyword Google blog search.
- Scroll to the bottom (blogs) or set up a keyword-specific Google Alert.
- Monitor your email alerts as they roll in.
- Think out of the box -- not just your company name, but competitors and keywords.

The person assigned to do this is: _____.

Deadline to complete: _____, 201_.

INTERNET RESOURCES

Google Alerts

According to Google, Google Alerts are email updates of the latest relevant Google results (web, news, etc.) based on your queries. Enter a search query you wish to monitor. You will see a preview of the type of results you'll receive. So basically define a) your company name, b) your target keywords, and/or c) your competitors' names and then Google will alert you to things it finds such as blog posts, news stories, or web pages on those topics.
http://www.google.com/alerts

Google Blog Search

Another way to use Google alerts is to do a Google blog search for your company name, competitors' names, and/or keywords. Then scroll to the bottom and you'll see a link to"'create a Google Alert" for this keyword. It's an easy way to see what you'll get before you set it up in Google Alerts.
http://www.google.com/blogsearch

Gmail

Gmail is Google's own email service. Since Google Alerts is a Google product, the easiest way to manage it is to use another Google product, Gmail, for your Google Alerts. We recommend signing up for Gmail first, and then activating Google Alerts. Just drink the Google Kool-Aid -- it makes life easier!
http://www.gmail.com/

PRESS RELEASES

USE FREE AND PAID NEWS RELEASE SERVICES FOR BUZZ, SOCIAL MENTIONS, AND LINKS.

PROMOTE YOUR COMPANY!

- Google loves news, and Google loves sites with frequent news updates.
- Leverage free and paid services for near-instant social mentions, links, buzz.
- Identify bloggers, Twitterers and others who might repost your news.

DESCRIPTION: News is one of the most powerful techniques that you can use for Search Engine Optimization. Why? First, Google loves new content. Generating new press releases in a systematic way means Google will see your site as having "fresh content," as opposed to sites that lack fresh content. Second, when you use news as an SEO tactic, there are syndication services available -- both free and paid -- that allow you to build instant SEO-friendly links and social mentions. Third, generating news gives you the opportunity to identify bloggers and Twitterers who might be interested in your news. So news presents many, many wonderful SEO opportunities.

BEST FOR: All organizations.

DO THIS: Monthly.

TIME TO COMPLETE: Each time, a few hours or less.

HOW IMPORTANT IS THIS IS TO YOUR BUSINESS?

< **Not Important – Neutral – Very Important** >
☐   ☐☐☐   ☐

WHAT GRADE DO YOU GIVE YOUR COMPANY ON THIS TASK?

☐ **Not Relevant | Grade: < F –D – C – B – A >**

TO-DO'S

- Identify timely, SEO-friendly news topics.
- Post SEO-friendly news on your website as press releases.
- Syndicate your news through free or paid news services.
- Identify bloggers and Twitterers who might be interested in your press release.

The person assigned to do this is: _____.

Deadline to complete: _____, 201_.

INTERNET RESOURCES

PR Log

PRLOG.org is one of the very best free services for press release syndication. First, register for a free account with your business email. Second, upload your news release with an active link to your website. Finally, tag it with the appropriate keywords.
http://www.prlog.org/

PRWeb

PRWeb, run by Vocus, is perhaps the best paid SEO-friendly service. For approximately $199, you can generate an SEO-friendly press release. They then send your news to major search engines like Google, Yahoo! News, and Bing as well as 30,000+ journalists and bloggers. They also have subscribers and host the release on their own site, with a nice SEO-friendly link.
http://www.prweb.com/

How to Syndicate a Press Release (Part I)

In this video on how to write a good SEO-friendly press release, I -- Jason McDonald -- explain six basic steps, starting with SEO keyword research, going through writing a strong TITLE tag and keyword-heavy text for the release, and ending up with how to cross-link your press release to your home page for the best Search Engine Optimization.
http://bit.ly/Pd8xZ8

How to Syndicate a Press Release for SEO on Free Press Release Services (Part II)

Once you have a press release up on your website, what do you do with it? The answer: syndication! In this video, learn about using freeand paid press release services to syndicate your press release. News websites, blogs, portals, even Twitter can pick up your news release, getting you lots of inbound links (good for SEO) and social mentions (also good for SEO!).
http://bit.ly/NI89BE

LINK SCULPT

LINK SCULPT YOUR HOME PAGE, SITE NAVIGATION, AND EXTERNAL LINKS TO YOUR WEBSITE.

CREATE STRONG SEO CONTENT!

- Google pays great attention to keyword phrases in links.
- Link sculpting means architecting how "link juice" flows amongst your pages.
- Link sculpting occurs both on your own site and via external links to your site.

DESCRIPTION: Google pays keen attention to links on the Internet. If website A links to website B around the phrase "top SEO Training," then Google interprets this link from site A to site B as a vote that site A should be placed higher on a Google search page for the phrase "top SEO training." Link sculpting is the concept of identifying your target keywords, soliciting external links using those keyword phrases, and doing the same thing on your own website. It is particularly important to pay attention to how your home page "links down" to subordinate pages (the A HREF tag should focus on a keyword target) as well as to your site navigation. Keyword heavy site navigation is part of link sculpting. Finally, don't overdo it! Over-sculpting internal or external links can be a red flag to Google that you are spamming. So have some variety in your link phrases and be focused: choose no more than five phrases that matter to your SEO.

BEST FOR: All organizations.

DO THIS: One time.

TIME TO COMPLETE: A few hours or less.

HOW IMPORTANT IS THIS IS TO YOUR BUSINESS?

< Not Important – Neutral – Very Important >
☐　　☐☐☐　　☐

WHAT GRADE DO YOU GIVE YOUR COMPANY ON THIS TASK?

☐ **Not Relevant | Grade: < F –D – C – B – A >**

TO-DO'S

- Identify your target keywords and key phrases.
- Set up internal site navigation, so that A HREF tags contains the target keywords.
- Set up "one click" links from your home page down to keyword-rich landing pages.
- Solicit external links around your target phases.
- Remember not to overdo it! Link sculpting that is "too perfect" can actually be negative!

The person assigned to do this is: _____.

Deadline to complete: _____, 201_.

INTERNET RESOURCES

The NOFOLLOW attribute
Wikipedia explains the'"nofollow" attribute for links. Originally created to fight blog spam, the attribute has had a long and, some would say troubled, history with respect to link sculpting.
http://en.wikipedia.org/wiki/Nofollow

WORDPRESS SEO

INSTALL WORDPRESS SEO PLUGINS

CREATE STRONG SEO CONTENT!

- WordPress is the No. 1 blogging platform.
- If you are using WordPress, install an SEO plugin.
- If you aren't using WordPress, check your blog output for SEO best practices

DESCRIPTION: WordPress may be the No. 1 blogging platform, but WordPress right out of the box isn't perfect for SEO. One challenge is getting SEO-friendly TITLE tags out of WordPress, especially if you want to have a different, shorter, more keyword-heavy TITLE for Google and a longer, more elegant HEADLINE for your users. A second challenge is the META DESCRIPTION tag -- WordPress themes often do not include a unique and accurate META DESCRIPTION tag for all blog posts. Installing an SEO plugin for WordPress helps fix these problems. Then as you write blog posts, be sure to verify that the TITLE and META DESCRIPTION are coming out in the HTML output appropriately. If you are not using WordPress, be sure to verify the same -- each blog post should have a unique and accurate TITLE and META DESCRIPTION tag.

BEST FOR: All organizations.

DO THIS: One time.

TIME TO COMPLETE: A few hours or less.

HOW IMPORTANT IS THIS IS TO YOUR BUSINESS?

< **Not Important – Neutral – Very Important** >
☐   ☐☐☐   ☐

WHAT GRADE DO YOU GIVE YOUR COMPANY ON THIS TASK?

☐ **Not Relevant | Grade: < F –D – C – B – A >**

TO-DO'S

- If you don't already have a blog, get one (WordPress.org preferred).
- Select a hosting service and install WordPress.
- Install one of the SEO Plugins for WordPress.
- Verify your HTML output is SEO-friendly (TITLE and META DESCRIPTION tags).
- Even if you are not using WordPress, verify your HTML output is SEO-friendly!

The person assigned to do this is: _____.

Deadline to complete: _____, 201_.

INTERNET RESOURCES

WordPress

WordPress is the dominant blogging platform and one of the best for SEO. If you don't have a blog already, download and install a WordPress blog from WordPress.org, using the hosting service and domain name of your choice. There is also a rich ecosystem of WordPress consultants and web designers who can help you customize WordPress themes.
http://www.wordpress.org/

Meta Tag Analyzer

SeoCentro designed this Meta Tag analysis tool to help webmasters analyze their web pages. This tool analyzes not only the Meta Tags but also where your keywords are positioned, and supplies you with information on keyword density. When using Firefox, use CTRL+F to highlight your keywords in the result. In doing so, you can quickly check to see if a target keyword is well positioned vis-a-vis important tags like the TITLE or META DESCRIPTION tag.
http://www.seocentro.com/tools/search-engines/metatag-analyzer.html

LEARN FROM GOOGLE

IDENTIFY AND USE OFFICIAL GOOGLE LEARNING SEO RESOURCES.

LEARN SOME TIPS, TRICKS OR SECRETS!

- Google has a wealth of SEO information such as forums, help files, and blogs.
- Unfortunately, nothing ties together these disparate resources.
- Bookmark these resources as your 24/7 Google help resource.

DESCRIPTION: Google is the world's best search engine, but it is not an education company. That said, Google produces some impressive learning sites on how search works, what SEO is, and how AdWords can be a part of an effective Internet marketing strategy. Set aside some quality time to bookmark, read, and refer to the impressive learning resources hidden in the Googleplex that can explain both general SEO issues and specific SEO questions as they arise. Don't forget the obvious -- if you have a burning question, just Google it! Once you can frame a question, simply typing that question into Google can be one of the easiest ways to find the answer. If you don't ask, you don't learn!

BEST FOR: All organizations.

DO THIS: As often as possible.

TIME TO COMPLETE: A few hours or less.

HOW IMPORTANT IS THIS IS TO YOUR BUSINESS?

< Not Important – Neutral – Very Important >
☐   ☐☐☐   ☐

WHAT GRADE DO YOU GIVE YOUR COMPANY ON THIS TASK?

☐ **Not Relevant | Grade: < F –D – C – B – A >**

TO-DO'S

- Practice searching Google for answers to SEO questions.
- Identify the various Google help resources.
- Identify, bookmark, and use the various Google blogs.
- Identify, bookmark, and use the various Google YouTube channels.
- Don't forget official Google forums for webmasters and SEO types.

The person assigned to do this is: _____.

Deadline to complete: _____, 201_.

INTERNET RESOURCES

Google Help Files

Directory of all help on Google, both for users and webmasters. A good starting point when you are really stumped!
http://support.google.com/?hl=en#show-more

Google Analytics IQ Lessons

If you are using Google Analytics, this is a must-see treasure trove of information on how to use that powerful platform. Ironically, it can be very difficult to jump from Google Analytics over to the Google IQ Lessons site. Only Google knows why they made it so difficult. That said, check out the topics and videos here. If you are really serious, you can study and get qualified as an Analytics Expert!
http://www.google.com/intl/en/analytics/iq.html?

Google Webmaster Help

Webmaster essentials from Google. Includes Google's official statements on SEO. To be taken with a grain of salt, because Google obviously has a huge vested interest in no one understanding how its algorithms work and thus being able to "manipulate" search results. But the help files for webmasters are here -- especially useful on webmaster issues like robots.txt, sitemaps, xml sitemaps and other "best practice'" for webmasters.
http://www.google.com/support/webmasters/

Google Business Channel on Youtube

A little hard to navigate. But poke around a while and you'll find some real gems of videos here on AdWords and Google in general. The Google channel on Youtube is where Google posts interviews, how to's, and other informative videos on how to use AdWords and Google Analytics. It is, unfortunately, not coordinated with other Google Youtube channels such as the Analytics channel.
http://www.youtube.com/user/GoogleBusiness

FREE SEO WEBINARS

ATTEND A FREE SEO EVENT.

LEARN SOME TIPS, TRICKS OR SECRETS!

- Many organizations, including Google, have free SEO webinars.
- Attend a free webinar to learn the basics, or keep up with the newest stuff.
- Pay attention to key blogs and websites to stay informed of new SEO trends.

DESCRIPTION: SEO, or Search Engine Optimization, is all about getting to the top of Google for free. Many organizations, including Google and my company, the JM Internet Group, often host free webinars on SEO. Many are not very good, but a few are quite informative. As part of your learning strategy, pay attention to key venues and organizations that host SEO events. Sign up for their email alerts, Twitter feeds, RSS feeds, or other ways to learn when and on what topic they will be hosting SEO events.

BEST FOR: All organizations.

DO THIS: As often as possible.

TIME TO COMPLETE: Each time, an hour or less.

HOW IMPORTANT IS THIS IS TO YOUR BUSINESS?

    < Not Important – Neutral – Very Important >
    ☐   ☐☐☐   ☐

WHAT GRADE DO YOU GIVE YOUR COMPANY ON THIS TASK?

☐ **Not Relevant | Grade: < F –D – C – B – A >**

TO-DO'S

- Identify interesting SEO webinars.
- Sign up and show up at a free SEO event.
- Sign up for email alerts, RSS feeds, or social media feeds on SEO events.

The person assigned to do this is: _____.

Deadline to complete: _____, 201_.

INTERNET RESOURCES

Top Ten Free Tools for Google/SEO

I'm proud to say that the JM Interneet Group produces one of the most popular free webinars on search engine optimization. Our SEO/Top Ten Tools webinar identifies the best SEO tools available. This webinar leads you through the basics of SEO and explains each and every tool. Attendees get a free copy of the famous SEO Toolbook, which contains hundreds of free SEO tools.
http://www.jm-seo.org/free/index.html

SEOMoz Free Webinars

SEOMoz is one of the leading blogs and portals on SEO, including some amazing free and paid tools for SEO. Their experts share some of that knowledge in free webinars. Check them out and learn!
http://www.seomoz.org/webinars

Hubspot Free Marketing Webinars

Hubspot is one of the better, if more expensive, services out there to help you with your SEO. They call it "inbound marketing," meaning that you can reach customers at the moment when they are looking for you or your products or services. They have many webinars or other free events (they do tend to be a bit salesy, however).
http://www.hubspot.com/marketing-webinars/

SEOMoz -- Whiteboard Fridays

Another great resource from SEOMoz! These are more YouTube videos than true webinars, but they are among the best in the business. Sign up for and show up for a "Whiteboard Friday." These informative events take an SEO topic, such as why videos appear at the top of YouTube searches, and explain them in detail. What's really great is that they tend to be very factual and not at all salesy.
http://www.seomoz.org/blog/category/33

SEO TRADE SHOWS

FOLLOW AND ATTEND THE MAJOR SEO INDUSTRY TRADE SHOWS.

LEARN SOME TIPS, TRICKS OR SECRETS!

- Trade shows and conferences are an opportunity to learn new trends in SEO.
- The major SEO trade shows travel across major cities.
- Many times, the free keynotes are as or more informative than the paid sessions!

DESCRIPTION: Learning the latest trends in SEO should become part of your weekly or monthly ritual. Reading the major SEO blogs and publications is one good way to do this, especially using Google Reader. Another way is to try to attend major SEO trade conferences, with the two most important being the SES Conference and its competitor, the SMX conference. If you are a hardcore SEO, the SEOMoz conference is also very good, albeit very technical. Fortunately, most of these shows travel across the USA and Canada, so bookmark their websites and watch for them to be near you. Even if you don't attend the paid conferences, many of the free events can be quite informative. Once you know the basics of SEO from a book or class, the conferences excel at the esoterica and latest debates. They are not, however, quite as helpful for beginners.

BEST FOR: Local Businesses.

DO THIS: As often as possible.

TIME TO COMPLETE: Each time, an hour or less.

HOW IMPORTANT IS THIS IS TO YOUR BUSINESS?

< Not Important – Neutral – Very Important >
☐   ☐☐☐   ☐

WHAT GRADE DO YOU GIVE YOUR COMPANY ON THIS TASK?

☐ **Not Relevant | Grade: < F –D – C – B – A >**

TO-DO'S

- Learn about the major SEO conferences.
- Pay attention to when they will be in a city near you.
- Register and attend at least the free sessions.
- Consider purchasing a paid conference pass, if you have the budget to do so.

The person assigned to do this is: _____.

Deadline to complete: _____, 201_.

INTERNET RESOURCES

Search Engine Strategies (SES) Conference

SES is the leading global event series about search and social marketing. Focusing on tactics and best practices, SES events bring together thought leaders and industry experts -- from private consultants to representatives from the search engines themselves -- to provide you with the skills to succeed in online marketing.
http://sesconference.com/

SMX - Search Marketing Expo

Attend SMX for tactics to increase website traffic, conversions...and sales! Register early to reserve your spot and save with Super Early Bird rates. Choose from over 50 sessions on search engine marketing topics including search engine optimization (SEO), paid search advertising, local/mobile search and social media marketing on Facebook, YouTube and Twitter.
http://searchmarketingexpo.com/

MozCon

Bringing you the brightest minds in search, social, inbound marketing, and more, MozCon is known for its dynamic, advanced content and idea-filled sessions. Roger, the Mozbot, can't wait to see you. Amazing content from industry leaders. Actionable tips and deep insights. Three days and one amazing experience.
http://www.seomoz.org/mozcon

PubCon

Supported by the industry's leading businesses, exhibitors and sponsors involved in social media, Internet marketing, search engines, and online advertising, PubCon Las Vegas 2012 will offer a week-long look at the future of technology presented by over 200 of the world's best speakers in more than 100 bold cutting-edge sessions.
http://www.pubcon.com/

LOCAL REVIEWS

ASK FOR REVIEWS ON GOOGLE+ LOCAL, YELP, ETC.

PROMOTE YOUR COMPANY!

- You don't ask, you don't get!
- Systematically asking for reviews is the No. 1 way to get reviews.
- The more reviews, the better you show on relevant Google, Yelp, etc., searches.

DESCRIPTION: "You don't ask, you don't get!" Or so the saying goes. It's certainly true in marketing. With the advent of SEO in general and local SEO in particular (think Google Places, Yelp, or Citysearch), reviews are a critical part of effective Internet marketing. First, the more reviews you have, the better you will show up on the "search function" of Google/Google+ Local, Yelp, or Citysearch. All review-based sites clearly reward companies that have more reviews, and even more so, companies that have reviews from established reviewers who use your keywords in their reviews. Second, customers often select a company based on online reviews. So having reviews leads to more customers, even if those customers find you by a means other than SEO. Finally, reviews encourage a virtuous circle. The more reviews, the better you show on search, the more customers, the more reviews -- and so on and so forth. So get reviews! The easiest way to start is to ASK for reviews. After each customer experience, have your sales person ask that customer if he or she is happy with the service or product. If so, then ask for a review. If not, fix the problem before they write a negative review. "You don't ask, you don't get!"

BEST FOR: Local Businesses.

DO THIS: As often as possible.

TIME TO COMPLETE: Each time, an hour or less.

HOW IMPORTANT IS THIS IS TO YOUR BUSINESS?

    < Not Important – Neutral – Very Important >
    ☐   ☐☐☐   ☐

WHAT GRADE DO YOU GIVE YOUR COMPANY ON THIS TASK?

    ☐ **Not Relevant | Grade: < F –D – C – B – A >**

TO-DO'S

- Claim your free listings on Google+ Local, Yelp, and Citysearch.
- Set up a sales process whereby at the end of the process customers are asked if they are satisfied.
- Incentivize/motivate your sales staff to ask for reviews in person.
- Set up an email system to ask for reviews a few days after a successful sale.
- Monitor your SEO performance on the larger review sites.

The person assigned to do this is: _____.

Deadline to complete: _____, 201_.

GOOGLE ANALYTICS

SET UP AND UTILIZE GOOGLE'S FREE WEB METRICS PLATFORM.

MEASURE OR MONITOR YOUR PERFORMANCE!

- Google Analytics is the No. 1 free metrics platform.
- Set up your website on Google Analytics ASAP.
- Create baseline metrics in Analytics for inbound traffic and user behavior.

DESCRIPTION: Google Analytics is the premier, free platform for Web metrics. If you haven't done so already, go to Google Analytics and register for your free account. Place the required Javascript code on all pages of your website. Next, as you begin to receive data, learn how to use Google Analytics to measure inbound traffic from sources such as direct, referrals, and organic SEO searches. You can also define goals in Analytics such as registrations or purchases, and use Advanced Segments to slice and dice customers based on attributes such as lead origin (organic vs. paid advertising), geographic (Texas vs. California), or even device (mobile vs. desktop). The sky is the limit, even if Analytics can be a bit daunting. Fortunately, there are some great learning sites to help you master Google Analytics.

BEST FOR: All organizations.

DO THIS: Monthly.

TIME TO COMPLETE: An hour or less.

HOW IMPORTANT IS THIS IS TO YOUR BUSINESS?

< Not Important – Neutral – Very Important >
☐   ☐☐☐   ☐

WHAT GRADE DO YOU GIVE YOUR COMPANY ON THIS TASK?

☐ **Not Relevant | Grade: < F –D – C – B – A >**

TO-DO'S

- Set up your free Google Analytics account.
- Place the required Javascript code on all pages and verify.
- Understand basic Analytics such as traffic origin.
- Define goals such as registrations or sales.
- Use Advanced Segments to slice and dice your potential customers.

The person assigned to do this is: _____.

Deadline to complete: _____, 201_.

INTERNET RESOURCES

Google Analytics

Google Analytics is the enterprise-class web analytics solution that gives you rich insights into your website traffic and marketing effectiveness. Powerful, flexible and easy-to-use features now let you see and analyze your traffic data in an entirely new way. With Google Analytics, you're more prepared to write better-targeted ads, strengthen your marketing initiatives and create higher converting websites.
http://www.google.com/analytics/

Google Analytics IQ Lessons

If you are using Google Analytics, this is a must-see treasure trove of information on how to use that powerful platform. Ironically, it can be very difficult to jump from Google Analytics over to the Google IQ Lessons site. Only Google knows why they made it so difficult. That said, check out the topics and videos here. If you are really serious, you can study and get qualified as an Analytics Expert!
http://www.google.com/intl/en/analytics/iq.html?

BLOG COMMENTING

IDENTIFY RELEVANT BLOGS AND COMMENT ON THEM.

PROMOTE YOUR COMPANY!

- The blogosphere is an amazing SEO resource, if used properly.
- Identify bloggers who blog about your keywords, company, or products.
- Reach out to bloggers with news items and content ideas.

DESCRIPTION: Blogging is perhaps the oldest form of social media. Bloggers write about topics that they are passionate about, and many of them will be writing on topics (read: keywords) that matter to you and your company. Identifying key influencers in your industry is an important marketing tactic; identifying key bloggers brings this tactic into the Internet age. Your primary research project is to identify bloggers who are writing about your keywords, about your company, and/or about your competitors. Build a list of bloggers and reach out to them with your news, new content ideas, and even guest blog post queries. Nurturing relationships with influential bloggers is a key tactic for creating SEO success.

BEST FOR: All organizations.

DO THIS: As often as possible.

TIME TO COMPLETE: Each time, an hour or less.

HOW IMPORTANT IS THIS IS TO YOUR BUSINESS?

< Not Important – Neutral – Very Important >

☐ ☐☐☐ ☐

WHAT GRADE DO YOU GIVE YOUR COMPANY ON THIS TASK?

☐ Not Relevant | Grade: < F –D – C – B – A >

TO-DO'S

- Know your SEO keyword targets.
- Research and identify influential bloggers via Google blog search.
- Reach out to bloggers with your news or new content ideas.
- Consider offering a "guest blog post" on a relevant blog.
- Measure your blog results via Google Analytics referral data.

The person assigned to do this is: _____.

Deadline to complete: _____, 201_.

INTERNET RESOURCES

Google Blog Search

Blogs are an important SEO opportunity, both as examples of good content and as sources for link building. Every important website should also have its own blog. Thankfully, Google has a powerful blog search. Access it directly, or from the main Google page, click on "more" and then "blogs." Enter your target keywords to find blogs that cover your industry.

http://www.google.com/blogsearch

IceRocket

IceRocket is a very good blog search engine. Don't miss the Trend Tool, which allows you to enter a keyword and watch trends.

http://www.icerocket.com/

Topsy

Topsy is a real-time search engine for Twitter, blogs, and the Web. You can also search the web and videos. VERY important: You can use this to input a URL (say, jm-seo.org or chipestimate.com) and see how frequently that URL and its sub-URLs have been tweeted, so it's a great way to see your social shares!

http://topsy.com/

Technorati

Technorati collects, organizes, and distributes the global online conversation. Founded as the first blog search engine, Technorati has expanded to a full service media company.

http://www.technorati.com/

GOOGLE ANALYTICS LEARNING

WATCH INFORMATIVE GOOGLE VIDEOS ON HOW TO USE ANALYTICS.

MEASURE OR MONITOR YOUR PERFORMANCE!

- Google Analytics is the No. 1 free platform for metrics.
- Learn how to use it effectively.
- Got a Google Analytics question? Watch an informative free video.

DESCRIPTION: Google Analytics is the premier, free platform for Web analytics. The Google Analytics platform, however, is anything but easy. Keywords, page views, bounce rate, Advanced Segments, Referrer Websites, SEO, and even social media -- so many metrics, so little time! Beyond the help function in Google Analytics (located at the top right of each page), did you know that Google produces a free online learning center, called Google IQ Tests? And did you know that for $50, you can take a test to be officially certified by Google Analytics? Now you do!

BEST FOR: All businesses.

DO THIS: As needed.

TIME TO COMPLETE: Each time, a few hours or less.

HOW IMPORTANT IS THIS IS TO YOUR BUSINESS?

< Not Important – Neutral – Very Important >
☐   ☐☐☐   ☐

WHAT GRADE DO YOU GIVE YOUR COMPANY ON THIS TASK?

☐ **Not Relevant | Grade:** < F –D – C – B – A >

TO-DO'S

- Sign up for Google Analytics.
- Log on to the Google Analytics IQ Tests website.
- Take their online video courses.
- If you like, pay $50 and be certified in Google Analytics.
- Be smug, since you not only know where Google IQ Tests are located, but you've been certified!

The person assigned to do this is: _____.

Deadline to complete: _____, 201_.

INTERNET RESOURCES

Google Analytics IQ Tests

Google Analytics is an amazing platform for metrics and analytics on your website or blog -- but it can be confusing. Fortunately, Google produces this amazing online learning center of videos and quizzes to learn about Google Analytics, and even test your knowledge. For $50, you can even take an official test and be Google certified! Ironically, you can't easily get from Google Analytics to the Google Analytics IQ Tests, but if you know where to look on the Web, you can find it yourself.
http://www.google.com/intl/en/analytics/iq.html

WEBMASTER TOOLS

SET UP WEBMASTER TOOLS IN GOOGLE AND BING.

MEASURE OR MONITOR YOUR PERFORMANCE!

- Gain useful data on how the search engines perceive your website.

- Leverage powerful reporting and analytics.

- Get advance warning of web issues before they hurt your SEO traffic.

DESCRIPTION: Have you ever wondered what Google (or Bing, for that matter) knows about your website or what your relationship is to Google? Succeeding at SEO requires many things to go right, but the starting point is being well-indexed by Google or Bing. Both search companies provide a free resource aptly named "Webmaster Tools." Once you sign up for it by placing a little confirming code on your website to authenticate yourself as the rightful owner of yourwebsite.com, you'll begin get inside information on how your site is indexed and tracked by Google or Bing -- all for free! Since Google is the bigger of the two, we'll focus on Google's Webmaster Tools in the steps below.

BEST FOR: All organizations.

DO THIS: One time.

TIME TO COMPLETE: A few hours or less.

HOW IMPORTANT IS THIS IS TO YOUR BUSINESS?

< Not Important – Neutral – Very Important >
☐   ☐☐☐   ☐

WHAT GRADE DO YOU GIVE YOUR COMPANY ON THIS TASK?

☐ Not Relevant | Grade: < F –D – C – B – A >

TO-DO'S

- Sign up for Webmaster Tools (at least for Google).
- Verify ownership.
- Login to Webmaster Tools.
- Check out important attributes such as pages indexed, proper TITLE or DESCRIPTION tags, and site speed.
- Fix any problems that are identified.

The person assigned to do this is: _____.

Deadline to complete: _____, 201_.

INTERNET RESOURCES

Google's Webmaster Tools

Webmaster tools is Google's "insider scoop" program for Webmasters and small business-people who want to monitor their relationship with Google. This free service allows you to understand how many pages of your site are indexed by Google, as well as giving you important information on HTML tags, site health, and even site speed. https://www.google.com/webmasters/tools/

Bing's Webmaster Tools

While Bing is a much smaller search engine than Google, it, too, provides a Webmaster Tools program. You can check how Bing perceives your site. One of its nifty features is its link-building technology; you can monitor inbound links to your site over time. http://www.bing.com/toolbox/webmaster/

TRENDING SEARCHES

IDENTIFY TRENDING SEARCHES FOR BLOG AND WEBSITE CONTENT.

LEARN SOME TIPS, TRICKS OR SECRETS!

- Trending searches are new, rising searches showing what's buzzing.
- If you can identify them early, trending searches make great blog posts.
- Catching a trending search is as much an art as it is a science.

DESCRIPTION: A trending, rising, or "hot" search is a search that is at the beginning of the news cycle. It is often a news announcement, radical new product, or something just really exciting. A few people hear about it, and they tweet it or share it to their followers. Then others find out about it, yet still don't understand what it is -- so they turn to Google. Trending searches are hot SEO opportunities, because if you can identify a trend early, you can blog about it early and more easily get to the top of Google. Trending search research goes hand-in-hand with newsjacking.

BEST FOR: All organizations.

DO THIS: Daily.

TIME TO COMPLETE: A few hours or less.

HOW IMPORTANT IS THIS IS TO YOUR BUSINESS?

< Not Important – Neutral – Very Important >
☐   ☐☐☐   ☐

WHAT GRADE DO YOU GIVE YOUR COMPANY ON THIS TASK?

☐ **Not Relevant | Grade:** < F –D – C – B – A >

TO-DO'S

- Monitor tools for relevant trending searches in your industry.
- Once you see a good trend, attempt to blog about it quickly.
- Use SEO techniques to dominate Google for a trending search.
- Don't forget to have a defined action such as a "registration" or "sale" on your landing page.
- Repeat frequently; the best bloggers are trend watchers.

The person assigned to do this is: _____.

Deadline to complete: _____, 201_.

INTERNET RESOURCES

Google Insights for Search

See what the world is searching for with this free tool from Google. It is mainly of use in watching search trends. Enter a keyword and the dates, and watch trends emerge (or fail to emerge) across time. Try "cash for clunkers" to see the rise and fall of that program. Try "flowers" to see the peaks around Mother's Day and Valentine's Day. If your business possibly has trends in time, use this tool to observe them.
http://www.google.com/insights/search/#

Google Hot Trends

Google Hot Trends are the hottest searches worldwide for any given day. Not that useful for most of us, but still provides insights into what people are searching for.
http://www.google.com/trends/hottrends

IceRocket Popular

Most popular posts on IceRocket, which monitors the blogosphere for trends.
http://www.icerocket.com/popular/posts

Most Emailed News

What gets emailed is often a trend. Again, this site shares items that are more mass market. But they are food for thought for you -- what might be trending in your industry, and how can you hop on it quickly as a blogger?media company.
http://mostemailednews.com/

GOOGLE +1 BUTTON AND GOOGLE+ BADGE

SET UP THE +1 BUTTON AND GOOGLE+ BADGE ON YOUR WEBSITE.

PROMOTE YOUR COMPANY!

- Google+ is Google's latest social network, similar to Facebook.
- The Google +1 Button allows users to "recommend" an individual page.
- The Google+ Badge allows users to "circle" your business page directly.

DESCRIPTION: Google+ is Google's latest social network, similar to, yet different from, Facebook. Users "circle" your business page (or your personal page), thereby building your audience and, to some extent, your SEO performance on Google natural search. The Google +1 button allows a user to "+1" an individual web page, thereby telling their Google+ friends (and Google) that your site is cool and important. The Google+ Badge, in contrast, allows your users to "circle" your personal or corporate Google+ page in one quick click.

BEST FOR: All organizations.

DO THIS: One time.

TIME TO COMPLETE: A few hours or less.

HOW IMPORTANT IS THIS IS TO YOUR BUSINESS?

< **Not Important – Neutral – Very Important** >
☐   ☐☐☐   ☐

WHAT GRADE DO YOU GIVE YOUR COMPANY ON THIS TASK?

☐ **Not Relevant | Grade:** < F –D – C – B – A >

TO-DO'S

- Set up your personal (or corporate) Google+ Page.

- Get the code for the Google +1 Button (so users can "recommend" a page).

- Get the code for the Google+ Badge (so users can "circle" your Google+ page).

- Implement the code on the relevant pages of your website.

- Promote Google+ in its own right and as a tool for Google SEO.

The person assigned to do this is: _____.

Deadline to complete: _____, 201_.

INTERNET RESOURCES

Google+ for Business

Here is Google's official gateway page to both the +1 button and the Google+ Badge. Get the code for either (or both) and add to your website.
http://www.google.com/+/business/promote.html

TWEET URLS

IDENTIFY TOP TWITTERERS AND GET THEM TO TWEET YOUR URLS.

PROMOTE YOUR COMPANY!

- Twitter is a powerful platform for URL sharing.
- Get powerful Twitterers to share your URLs and increase traffic to your website.
- Tweet your own URLs to increase Google pickup.

DESCRIPTION: Twitter is often thought of as the craziest, most useless social media site. Maybe it is. Maybe it isn't. But one thing is clear: Google and Bing pay a lot of attention to which URLs get shared on Twitter. Twitter is amazingly open, so the search engines can easily penetrate it to see what's a-Tweet. Think like Google or Bing -- if a URL is being tweeted, it must be important. So they had better go index that content, and even give it a little boost in terms of the search results. It's called a "social mention." Find people in your industry active on Twitter and incentivize them to tweet your new blog posts, your new press releases, your new products -- anything and everything new and happening on your website. Even if Twitter isn't a primary marketing vehicle for your company, getting your URLs tweeted can help you with your SEO.

BEST FOR: All organizations.

DO THIS: As often as possible.

TIME TO COMPLETE: A few hours or less.

HOW IMPORTANT IS THIS IS TO YOUR BUSINESS?

> **< Not Important – Neutral – Very Important >**
> ☐   ☐☐☐   ☐

WHAT GRADE DO YOU GIVE YOUR COMPANY ON THIS TASK?

> ☐ **Not Relevant | Grade: < F –D – C – B – A >**

TO-DO'S

- Set up your own Twitter account on Twitter.com.
- Tweet your URLs as you post new items to your blog, site, news releases, etc.
- Identify people who tweet on your keywords.
- Reach out to those powerful Twitterers, and ask them to tweet your URLs.

The person assigned to do this is: _____.

Deadline to complete: _____, 201_.

INTERNET RESOURCES

Twitter Advanced Search

If you don't know it already, Twitter is one of the darlings of social media. Now it might all be a big waste of time, and certainly is for some industries (not for others). Regardless, set up your free Twitter account, get some followers, and begin tweeting your new blog posts, new product announcements and other content. It's one tactic to get Google or Bing to pay attention. Use their advanced search feature for even more nuanced results. http://twitter.com/#!/search-home

Bing Social

Bing Social is an amazing free service to identify powerful Twitterers and Facebookers. Enter your target keywords, and find people who are tweeting on those topics. Then reach out to them to get them to tweet your own URLs (blog posts, new products, etc.). http://www.bing.com/social

Google Twitter Search

Google is the world's best search engine. Using the command site:twitter.com in the Google search engine, you can search Google by keyword. Simply know your keyword, and type site:google.com keyword into the search engine. For instance, to find people who Tweet on "organic food," type site:twitter.com "organic food" into the Google search bar. http://www.google.com/

GOOGLE SEO GUIDE

DOWNLOAD AND READ THE OFFICIAL GOOGLE GUIDE TO SEO.

LEARN SOME TIPS, TRICKS OR SECRETS!

- Don't miss Google's one and only official guide to "on page" SEO.
- Explains the top tips for including preferred tags and website structure.
- Useful for organizational politics, as the official guide to what Google wants.

DESCRIPTION: Google makes billions on AdWords, its paid advertising project. The Googleplex therefore spends many millions promoting AdWords as the solution to all Internet marketing problems. Not so with SEO, via which Google makes no money. You have to know where to look to find the Google gospel on SEO. The official Google SEO Guide succinctly explains what your organization should do in terms of page tags (TITLE tag, META DESCRIPTION tag, HEADER tags), URL structure, and website organization. It emphasizes writing good, well-structured SEO content. Finally, as an official Google guide, it is an authoritative source of how to put together an effective SEO website. If you meet internal staff resistance at your company around SEO, the Google guide can be a useful motivator for your team.

BEST FOR: All organizations.

DO THIS: One time.

TIME TO COMPLETE: A few hours or less.

HOW IMPORTANT IS THIS IS TO YOUR BUSINESS?

< **Not Important – Neutral – Very Important** >
☐   ☐☐☐   ☐

WHAT GRADE DO YOU GIVE YOUR COMPANY ON THIS TASK?

☐ **Not Relevant | Grade:** < F –D – C – B – A >

TO-DO'S

- Download the PDF version of the Google SEO Starter Guide.
- Read the guide, paying special attention to its "on page" recommendations.
- Share the guide with your SEO team.
- Implement its suggestions.
- Remember that it focuses primarily on "on page" SEO, and not "off page" SEO.

The person assigned to do this is: _____.

Deadline to complete: _____, 201_.

INTERNET RESOURCES

Google SEO Guide

Google's SEO guide is the quickest free "how to" guide to on-page SEO on the Internet. For bloggers and blogging, it provides quick tips like the importance of keywords in your TITLE tag and META DESCRIPTION tag, as well as the insight that having an image on the page with an SEO-friendly ALT attribute is a must.
http://bit.ly/cGsqb4

BLOG, BLOG, BLOG

CREATE SEO-FRIENDLY BLOG POSTS -- FREQUENTLY.

CREATE STRONG SEO CONTENT!

- Identify trending keywords as well as primary keywords that you target for SEO.
- Understand the basics of on-page SEO, and embed these keywords in blog posts.
- Create one-click links from your home page to your blog post.

DESCRIPTION: Blogs are one of the easiest, most powerful SEO tactics. Google loves blogs, because Google loves fresh content! Moreover, blogs provide you the opportunity to target specific keywords. Think of your website and major landing pages as the "anchor stores" at the shopping mall, and your blog posts as the boutiques. The former are focused on your major keyword areas, and the latter are focused on specific, micro-targeted keywords searches. Combining a laser focus on keywords with the freshness factor, blogs are one SEO opportunity you do not want to miss! Blog, blog, blog on your keywords, keywords, keywords!

BEST FOR: All organizations.

DO THIS: As often as possible.

TIME TO COMPLETE: Each time, an hour or less.

HOW IMPORTANT IS THIS IS TO YOUR BUSINESS?

< **Not Important – Neutral – Very Important** >
☐ ☐☐☐ ☐

WHAT GRADE DO YOU GIVE YOUR COMPANY ON THIS TASK?

☐ **Not Relevant | Grade:** < **F –D – C – B – A** >

TO-DO'S

- Set up your blog, using a free program like WordPress.
- Identify specific SEO keywords for each blog post.
- Embed the target keywords in your blog post TITLE tag and META DESCRIPTION tags.
- Write strong, keyword-heavy, SEO-friendly content.
- Don't forget your human audience -- blog on topics that potential customers want to read about.

The person assigned to do this is: _____.

Deadline to complete: _____, 201_.

INTERNET RESOURCES

Google SEO Guide

Google's SEO guide is the quickest free "how to" guide to on-page SEO on the Internet. For bloggers and blogging, it provides quick tips like the importance of keywords in your TITLE tag and META DESCRIPTION tag, as well as the insight that having an image on the page with an SEO-friendly ALT attribute is a must.
http://bit.ly/cGsqb4

Google SEO Keyword Tool

Use Google's keyword tool to identify high volume, high value keywords. The very first thing you should do when writing a blog post is to identify the keywords your customers are actually using.
https://adwords.google.com/o/KeywordTool

SEO All in One Plugin for WordPress

WordPress is not SEO-friendly right out of the box, so install one of the free plugins to help optimize the WordPress structure for search engine optimization issues.
http://wordpress.org/extend/plugins/all-in-one-seo-pack/

Yoast

Yoast is one of the newer plugins for WordPress. With much hype and fanfare, it's become one of the SEO favorites for WordPress.
http://yoast.com/

BUILD AN EMAIL LIST

LEVERAGE THE POWER OF EMAIL MARKETING BY BUILDING A LIST.

DEFINE YOUR DESIRED ACTIONS!

- Email marketing remains the most powerful marketing on the Internet.
- "You don't ask, you don't get." Ask people to sign up for your email newsletter!
- Be respectful of their needs by emailing only useful information.

DESCRIPTION: In this day of Twitter, Facebook, Google+ and of course SEO, people forget that the number-one application on the Internet remains email. Email marketing is the most powerful form of marketing on the Internet today, bar none. It is even more powerful than SEO. But how do you build an email list? "You don't ask, you don't get." So first, define WHY customers want to subscribe to your email alerts -- perhaps it's free offers, coupons or discounts, insider deals on your latest and greatest products, updates on new technology, or other information. Define something that your customers want or need, and then clarify on your website how they "sign up" for your email alerts or newsletter. SEO comes in by getting you to the top of Google, where potential customers then find your site and sign up.

BEST FOR: All organizations.

DO THIS: As often as possible.

TIME TO COMPLETE: A few hours or less.

HOW IMPORTANT IS THIS IS TO YOUR BUSINESS?

< **Not Important – Neutral – Very Important** >
☐   ☐☐☐   ☐

WHAT GRADE DO YOU GIVE YOUR COMPANY ON THIS TASK?

☐ **Not Relevant | Grade: < F –D – C – B – A >**

TO-DO'S

- Define why prospects or customers will want to get your emails.
- Create the content, such as email alerts or an email newsletter, that customers will want to get. Target SEO keywords and landing actions for your top SEO landing pages.
- Set up feeders on your website to register for email alerts or your newsletter.
- Verify that your signup process works.
- Email your customers in a respectful manner, sending them free and truly informative content.

The person assigned to do this is: _____.

Deadline to complete: _____, 201_.

INTERNET RESOURCES

Constant Contact

Constant Contact is one of the leading, and most heavily advertised, email management systems out there. Their software will manage your signups, unsubscribes, and other aspects of your email list. But, like all these services, they really do little to promote the list. That's your job. Don't miss their learning center -- it has some good, if salesy, information on email marketing.
http://www.constantcontact.com/

AWeber

AWeber is a competitor to Constant Contact. Known as a friendlier, more "customer-friendly" company, it also has a reputation as being better as an email response system. In that sense, it doesn't just manage your email list, but enables you to create a registration and response system for freebies like PDF downloads.
http://www.aweber.com/

SERP RANK

CHECK YOUR RANK ACROSS TARGET KEYWORDS.

MEASURE OR MONITOR YOUR PERFORMANCE!

- Customers search Google by keywords and prefer the top ten results.
- Results vary not just by keyword but also by geography.
- Universal search has made rank measurement more difficult.

DESCRIPTION: Customers search by keywords! They go to Google and type in phrases like "industrial fans for agriculture," or "best divorce attorney Dallas," or "herbal cures for sunburn." Does your company show up? What is your SERP (Search Engine Results Page) rank, not just for one keyword, or short tail (few word) keywords, but for long tail (many word) phrases? Effective SEO is all about knowing your keyword rank in a very detailed way. Then, just like for physical fitness, SEO "fitness" requires targeting your weaker keywords for SEO the same way a good athlete works on his or her weaknessses. Moreover, with universal search, results now vary by geography, personalization, and even social network! Systematic rank measurement remains a pivot point of effective SEO.

BEST FOR: All organizations.

DO THIS: Monthly.

TIME TO COMPLETE: Each time, a few hours or less.

HOW IMPORTANT IS THIS IS TO YOUR BUSINESS?

< **Not Important – Neutral – Very Important** >
☐   ☐☐☐   ☐

WHAT GRADE DO YOU GIVE YOUR COMPANY ON THIS TASK?

☐ **Not Relevant | Grade:** < F – D – C – B – A >

TO-DO'S

- Build out a detailed keyword worksheet with defined keyword lists.
- Per universal search, identify which searches matter -- traditional, Google+ Local, Video, etc.
- Use free tools to measure your rank systematically!
- Target your weaker keywords for more intense SEO.
- Added bonus: Feed your free rank data into your AdWords to save money!

The person assigned to do this is: _____.

Deadline to complete: _____, 201_.

INTERNET RESOURCES

Firefox RankChecker from SEOBook

Sign up for a free account, and you can use this tool to track your rank on Google. It only works on Firefox, so be sure to install Firefox first. Then follow these steps: First, input your domain; be sure to use lowercase. Second, input your keyword list. Third, input any competitor names. This handy tool will track your SERP rank (your position on a Google search). Ultimately you need to be at least in the top ten.
http://www.seobook.com/

Sitemapdoc's SERP Rank Checker

Sitemapdoc may have misnamed the tool using a RAS Syndrome problem, but nonetheless this easy-to-use rank checking tool makes their list one of the best easy SEO tools out there. Simply input your URL and a target keyword, and the tool quickly tells you your rank out of the top 64 sites. Easy, useful, free, and fun!
http://www.sitemapdoc.com/Serp-Rank.aspx

CuteRank

CuteRank is a download-only tool that will allow you to input ONE domain for free and then measure its rank over time. It's a pretty good tool, though not as useful as Firefox RankChecker.
http://cuterank.net/

YOUTUBE SEO

CREATE A YOUTUBE CHANNEL AND SEO OPTIMIZE YOUR YOUTUBE CONTENT.

PROMOTE YOUR COMPANY!

- Google owns YouTube, and Google favors YouTube videos in search results.
- Video is the No. 1 social media for engagement and viral spread.
- Setting up a simple YouTube channel can help your SEO in all aspects.

DESCRIPTION: Google owns YouTube, and users love video. In fact, YouTube is actually the Number 2 search engine (bigger than Bing!). In many searches on Google, you'll actually see YouTube videos on page one of your Google search results, depending on whether your keywords are in the video title, the video description, and video comments, plus how many views the video or channel has and how popular it is. So YouTube is an SEO opportunity in its own right! Setting up a YouTube channel is easy, and gives your organization the opportunity to host video content for free on Google. If all YouTube does is provide you with a few videos for your customers, that in and of itself is good. But it may do more. It may get some SEO traction for your video and channel.

BEST FOR: All organizations.

DO THIS: One time.

TIME TO COMPLETE: A few hours or less.

HOW IMPORTANT IS THIS IS TO YOUR BUSINESS?

< **Not Important – Neutral – Very Important** >
☐   ☐☐☐   ☐

WHAT GRADE DO YOU GIVE YOUR COMPANY ON THIS TASK?

☐ **Not Relevant | Grade:** < F –D – C – B – A >

TO-DO'S

- Set up a YouTube channel.
- Upload easy videos, such as trade show presentations or CEO "elevator pitches."
- SEO your YouTube videos, beginning with keyword-heavy video titles and descriptions.
- Embed YouTube video on your website pages to help drive user engagement.
- If appropriate, make SEO marketing for YouTube a goal in and of itself.

The person assigned to do this is: _____.

Deadline to complete: _____, 201_.

INTERNET RESOURCES

YouTube for Business
This is the official question-and-answer page for setting up a YouTube channel for business.
http://support.google.com/youtube/bin/static.py?hl=en&guide=2403720&page=guide.cs

YouTube Marketing Tips and Tricks -- How to Market Your Business on YouTube
Video is huge on the Internet, and YouTube is the dominant player. How do you find great videos to spur your own marketing ideas? How can you leverage YouTube either to promote your business or enhance your customer relationships? Is it all Justin Bieber and Lady Gaga, or is there more beneath the surface of YouTube? Watch this informative, fun introduction to YouTube as a marketing tool.
http://www.jm-seo.org/serious-humor/youtube-marketing.html

SOCIAL MEDIA PROFILES

CREATE SOCIAL MEDIA CHANNELS AND BACKLINK TO YOUR WEBSITE.

PROMOTE YOUR COMPANY!

- Citations and external links matter to Google.
- Social mentions are the new links to SEO.
- Shoot for a robust social media ecosystem that supports your SEO.

DESCRIPTION: Inbound links to your website are one of the major factors in successful SEO. Nowadays, however, both Google and Bing are paying close attention to "citations" and "social mentions." For "citations," they are referring to external websites such as Yelp or Citysearch that reference your company with keyword-heavy names, descriptions, and accurate addresses and phone numbers. For "social mentions," they are referring to your company listings on Google+, Twitter, Facebook, YouTube and other major social media sites. Claiming your listings is the first step toward an active social media ecoystem that also supports your SEO.

BEST FOR: All organizations.

DO THIS: One time.

TIME TO COMPLETE: A few hours or less.

HOW IMPORTANT IS THIS IS TO YOUR BUSINESS?

< **Not Important – Neutral – Very Important** >
☐   ☐☐☐   ☐

WHAT GRADE DO YOU GIVE YOUR COMPANY ON THIS TASK?

☐ **Not Relevant | Grade: < F –D – C – B – A >**

TO-DO'S

- Identify your logical social media targets.
- Go through the steps to identify, claim, and/or set up your free company profiles.
- Make sure your listings point back to your website.
- Cross-link your website to your social media profiles.
- Where possible, actively participate in relevant social media.

The person assigned to do this is: _____.

Deadline to complete: _____, 201_.

INTERNET RESOURCES

Twitter

Twitter, of course, is short, sweet posts on topics that matter to you and your customers. Setting up a free Twitter account and posting your blog updates or other content can help with SEO. Even better, grow a community of followers around you on Twitter.
http://twitter.com/

YouTube

YouTube is a social media site that many companies overlook. By creating a robust channel and uploading videos, you can create not only interesting content but backlinks to your website. With YouTube owned by Google, YouTube is very SEO-friendly.
http://www.youtube.com/

Facebook

If you don't have a corporate Facebook page, well -- get one. Having a Facebook page and active profile gets you into social media, and gets you some SEO capability, especially with Bing. Moreover, Google clearly pays some attention to Facebook posts and shares, so it certainly can't hurt for SEO.
http://www.facebook.com/

Google+ for Businesses

Google+ is the new kid on the social media block. Even better, its daddy is Google and so Google clearly rewards websites that support Google+ action. So set up both personal and corporate Google+ profiles, post, grow your circles, and cross-link to your website. If you are a local business, don't confuse Google+ with Google+ Local, as these are separate entities.
http://www.google.com/+/business/

HOME PAGE SEO

USE YOUR HOME PAGE AS THE PREMIER SEO GATEWAY TO YOUR WEBSITE.

CREATE STRONG SEO CONTENT!

- Google clearly rewards home pages in the fight to the top in SEO.
- Use your home page wisely, beginning with keyword-heavy text.
- Inbound links come to your home page, and your home page can flow link juice.

DESCRIPTION: "There's no place like home," as Dorothy reminded us in the Wizard of Oz. It seems that the folks at Google and Bing took this to heart -- search engines clearly reward SEO-friendly home pages in the competitive struggle to the top of the search engine results. An effective SEO strategy, therefore, places home page design at the center. Google clearly favors text-heavy home pages, so therefore write keyword-heavy text on your home page, yet be respectful of your human customers, who don't like clutter. Google also rewards anything on your site that is "one click" from your home page, so use your home page as a gateway to keyword-heavy landing pages. Finally, Google likes fresh, up-to-date websites, so freshen your home page with "one click" links to your latest blog posts and press releases.

BEST FOR: All organizations.

DO THIS: As needed.

TIME TO COMPLETE: A few hours or less.

HOW IMPORTANT IS THIS IS TO YOUR BUSINESS?

< **Not Important – Neutral – Very Important** >
☐ ☐☐☐ ☐

WHAT GRADE DO YOU GIVE YOUR COMPANY ON THIS TASK?

☐ **Not Relevant | Grade:** < F –D – C – B – A >

TO-DO'S

- Conduct a home page SEO audit.
- Is your home page text-heavy, with frequent occurrences of your keywords?
- Do keywords occur on your home page (not in comma, comma, comma format but real sentences)?
- Is your home page used as a "one click" gateway to defined landing pages?
- Is your home page freshened up by frequent postings of "one click" links to blogs and press releases?

The person assigned to do this is: _____.

Deadline to complete: _____, 201_.

FRESHNESS FIRST

FRESHEN YOUR WEBSITE WITH PRESS RELEASES AND FREQUENT NEW CONTENT.

CREATE STRONG SEO CONTENT!

- Freshness is a major factor in the Google SEO algorithm.
- Use new content to freshen your home page, blog, and entire website.
- Posting new content also trains Google to index your site more frequently.

DESCRIPTION: In this age of social media marketing and social mentions, people seem to forget that Google also values freshness. Assume Google is looking at two websites. Website A has a home page with new content and "one click" links to new blog posts, new press releases, and other fresh content. Website B has no new content. Google is going to be more sure that Website A is a living, breathing business, while Website B may be out of business altogether. In addition, Google realizes people who are searching often want new and fresh information.

BEST FOR: All organizations.

DO THIS: As often as possible.

TIME TO COMPLETE: A few hours or less.

HOW IMPORTANT IS THIS IS TO YOUR BUSINESS?

< Not Important – Neutral – Very Important >
☐   ☐☐☐   ☐

WHAT GRADE DO YOU GIVE YOUR COMPANY ON THIS TASK?

☐ **Not Relevant | Grade: < F –D – C – B – A >**

TO-DO'S

- Identify possible blog posts or news releases for regular updates.
- Write the blog posts or press releases, and post to your site.
- Add one-click links from your home page to the individual posts.
- Use the site: Command on Google and measure your indexing patterns.
- Consider using press releases services to add external syndication to the mix.

The person assigned to do this is: _____.

Deadline to complete: _____, 201_.

LOCAL SEO

CROSS-REFERENCE LOCAL LISTINGS AND YOUR WEBSITE CONSISTENTLY.

PROMOTE YOUR COMPANY!

- Beyond Google+ Local, other services like Yelp and Citysearch matter.
- Make sure that all your local listings match in terms of address and phone.
- Cross-reference from your website to your local listings.

DESCRIPTION: Local search is incredibly important for many businesses, and for most, Google+ Local is the number one resource to claim. Customers search Google for local businesses like pizza restaurants, lawyers, and roofing companies, to name just a few. But did you know that Google pays attention to your other listings as well? Being listed on Yelp, Citysearch, Yellowpages.com and other websites matters for local SEO. In addition, make sure that your website links back to your local listings (called "citations" in SEO) and that your local listings consistently have the same physical address and phone number for your business.

BEST FOR: Local businesses.

DO THIS: As needed.

TIME TO COMPLETE: More than a few hours.

HOW IMPORTANT IS THIS IS TO YOUR BUSINESS?

< Not Important – Neutral – Very Important >
☐   ☐☐☐   ☐

WHAT GRADE DO YOU GIVE YOUR COMPANY ON THIS TASK?

☐ **Not Relevant | Grade: < F –D – C – B – A >**

TO-DO'S

- Use Google to identify local listing services.
- Identify and claim all relevant local listing services.
- Make sure that your address and phone number are consistent across local listings.
- Link outward from your website to your local listing services.
- Get reviews not just on Google+ Local, but on other local services!

The person assigned to do this is: _____.

Deadline to complete: _____, 201__.

INTERNET RESOURCES

Google

Do a search on Google for your target keywords, such as "pizza restaurant NYC" or "roofing company Dallas." Identify the Google+ Local listings that are returned (usually they have the red balloons). Select one that has many reviews, and click over to its listing on Google+ Local (NOT its website). Then scroll to the bottom. There you will often see other non-Google local review sites such as Yelp, Citysearch, Urbanspoon, etc. Claim the listings for your organization on those sites.
http://www.google.com/

GetListed

GetListed is an all-in-one search for local listings. Input your company name and some other information, and it will quickly tell you if your listings exist. Then make sure that they are consistent. Consistency in what is termed "local citations" is very important to Google.
http://getlisted.org/

NAMING CONVENTIONS

USE KEYWORDS TO NAME URLS, DIRECTORIES, FILES, AND GRAPHICS.

CREATE STRONG SEO CONTENT!

- Keywords matter, and so do URLs -- so keyword-heavy URLs win!
- Many sites have very bad URL practices such as dynamic URLs, sessionID's, etc.
- Keyword URLs (file names) and graphics (jpgs, gifs, pngs) help your SEO.

DESCRIPTION: Google is a company of engineers, and engineers are nothing if not meticulous. If you read the Google SEO Guide, you'll detect a tone of organization above all things. Google wants websites that are clearly and hierarchically organized, with a great SEO-friendly home page, subdirectories that contain relevant items, and clear files names that tell the Googlebot what it will find inside. Moreover, Google clearly dislikes dynamic URLs and URLs that fail to contain keywords, as these can confuse the Googlebot and send it down a rabbit hole. So an SEO best practice is to have a consistent, keyword-themed site design, and to name your directories and files in a logical keyword fashion. Don't forget to name graphics after keywords as well. Of course, as with all things in life, moderation is important. Don't overdo it!

BEST FOR: All organizations.

DO THIS: One time.

TIME TO COMPLETE: Each time, a few hours or less.

HOW IMPORTANT IS THIS IS TO YOUR BUSINESS?

< Not Important – Neutral – Very Important >
☐　　　☐☐☐　　　☐

WHAT GRADE DO YOU GIVE YOUR COMPANY ON THIS TASK?

☐ **Not Relevant | Grade: < F –D – C – B – A >**

TO-DO'S

- Once you have defined your keywords, create a hierarchical map of your website.
- Inventory your existing website directories and file names -- do they reflect your keywords?
- Rewrite/rename directories and file names to be keyword-heavy.
- Avoid sessionID's, dynamic URLs, parameter URLs or any complicated URL schemes.
- Don't forget images! Google clearly prefers keyword-heavy image names.

The person assigned to do this is: _____.

Deadline to complete: _____, 201_.

INTERNET RESOURCES

Google SEO Guide (Section: Improve the structure of your URLs)
Google's SEO guide is the quickest free'"how to" guide to on page SEO on the Internet. For bloggers and blogging, it provides quick tips like the importance of keywords in your TITLE tag and META DESCRIPTION tag as well as the insight that having an image on the page with an SEO-friendly ALT attribute is a must.
http://bit.ly/cGsqb4

Dynamic URLs vs. Static URLs -- The Best Practice for SEO Is Still Clear
Landmark article by Rand Fishkin outlining best practices for URLs and how strongly static URLs outperform dynamic URLs, whatever Google might "officially" say. Being able to parse dynamic URLs is not the same thing as preferring dynamic URLs!
http://www.seomoz.org/blog/dynamic-urls-vs-static-urls-the-best-practice-for-seo-is-still-clear

GOOGLE+ LOCAL

FIND AND/OR CLAIM YOUR FREE, OFFICIAL GOOGLE+ LOCAL LISTING.

PROMOTE YOUR COMPANY!

- Google+ Local is integrated with local search and mobile search.
- Customers use Google to find and review local businessess.
- Your listing may exist, whether you like it or not. So claim it!

DESCRIPTION: Estimates are that over 20% of all search is local, and with the revolution of mobile phones (iPhones, Android, and others), search is becoming more local every day. Moreover, local searches -- for local pizza restaurants, attorneys, dog groomers, roofers, and everything else local -- are often transactional "buy" searches. So if you have a local business, claiming your free listing on Google+ Local (formerly Google Places) is a major, major must-do activity. It's pretty easy, especially if the phone number that Google has matches your true phone number. Even if that's not the case, you can claim by postcard as well. Claim your listing, optimize it for your keywords, and get happy customers to review you. It's a major SEO tactic to get to the top of local search!

BEST FOR: Local businesses.

DO THIS: One time.

TIME TO COMPLETE: A few hours or less.

HOW IMPORTANT IS THIS IS TO YOUR BUSINESS?

< Not Important – Neutral – Very Important >
☐   ☐☐☐   ☐

WHAT GRADE DO YOU GIVE YOUR COMPANY ON THIS TASK?

☐ Not Relevant | Grade: < F –D – C – B – A >

TO-DO'S

- Sign in to the Google account (perhaps your Gmail account) that you want to control your listing.
- Find your listing on Google+ Local via a maps.google.com search.
- Click on the "manage this page" icon on the far right.
- Follow the instructions to claim your listing.
- Upgrade your company name, description, and categories to be SEO keyword-heavy.

The person assigned to do this is: _____.

Deadline to complete: _____, 201_.

INTERNET RESOURCES

Google Maps

Ironically, Google maps is the easiest way to find your company listing, if it already exists. Simply go to maps.google.com, and type in your company name, city and state and perhaps your street address. Then, when you see your listing, don't click on your company name. Instead, click on the line that says "reviews." On the right side, you'll see "manage your listing." That's how you begin the process of claiming your listing.
http://maps.google.com/

Gmail

It's ideal for all your Google services, such as Google+ Local, Google Analytics, and Google Webmaster Tools, to be controlled through a single Gmail login. In fact, even if you already have a Gmail account, we recommend that you set up a "company Gmail" address for these services to avoid the potential problem of a personal employee address being used (and then lost if that person leaves the organization).
http://www.gmail.com/

Google Places

Google Places is the older name for Google+ Local, but it still controls the local listings. If you can't find your listing through the procedures above, go to the Google Places website and click on the far right side where it says "Get started now." The system will then guide you through the process of either identifying your listing, or if claimed, modifying your listing so that you have a strong keyword-heavy listing, description, and other information.
http://www.google.com/places/

Google+ Local (Google Places) Help

Here is the official Google help website for Google+ Local (formerly Google Places). Turn here for a relatively easy search-to-find system of news postings, tips, and other resources to troubleshoot any problems.
http://support.google.com/places/

LOCAL LISTINGS

CLAIM YOUR FREE LISTINGS ON ALL LOCAL SITES.

PROMOTE YOUR COMPANY!

- Your listing may exist, whether you want it or not.
- Claim your listing to optimize for SEO and add pictures, better content, etc.
- Participate in the ongoing conversation about YOUR business.

DESCRIPTION: : Upwards of 20% of all searches are local in nature, and most local search involves reviews. Hungry for pizza? Type "pizza" into the Google search engine, and Google happily returns companies that have not only claimed their free Google+ Local listing but also set up keyword-heavy listings, and solicited effective reviews from real customers. Similarly, Yelp and Citysearch as well as other big local search providers have a huge ecosystem of happy customers. For companies as diverse as pizza restaurants, attorneys, marriage counselors, roofing companies -- anyone and everyone that is a local business -- local search is huge. Gone are the days of the physical yellow pages. Here are the days of online search, and increasingly mobile search, to find the best local restaurants, attorneys, therapists, or anything else we need nearby. Your first step? Claim your FREE local listings.

BEST FOR: Local businesses.

DO THIS: One time.

TIME TO COMPLETE: A few hours or less.

HOW IMPORTANT IS THIS IS TO YOUR BUSINESS?

< **Not Important – Neutral – Very Important** >
☐   ☐☐☐   ☐

WHAT GRADE DO YOU GIVE YOUR COMPANY ON THIS TASK?

☐ **Not Relevant | Grade:** < F – D – C – B – A >

TO-DO'S

- Identify your free local listings on each service.
- Follow the steps to claim the listing (usually by phone confirmation).
- Make sure that your web address, physical address, and phone are all accurate.
- Revise your listing to be informative yet keyword heavy.

The person assigned to do this is: _____.

Deadline to complete: _____, 201_.

INTERNET RESOURCES

Google+ Local

Formerly called Google Places, Google+ Local is Google's local search service. First, find your listing on maps.google.com. Then claim your listing and revise it with a keyword heavy-title and description. Choose established categories from Google where possible.
http://www.google.com/places/

Yelp for Business

Yelp is a competitor to Google+ Local, started in San Francisco. Yelp tends to have a more loyal writer base than Google+ Local and is strong in many coastal markets such as San Francisco, Los Angeles, and New York City. Here's where you go to identify and claim your free Yelp listing..
https://biz.yelp.com/

Citysearch

Citysearch is a competitor to Yelp, a little less personal yet very important in many markets. Like Yelp and Google+, you can claim your free listing and then SEO optimize it for your target keywords.
http://www.citysearch.com/

Manta

Manta is a relative newcomer to the local business/small business listing space, but is heavily advertising itself. Like most services, it has a freemium model. You can claim your free listing and then they'll encourage you to pay for more. That may or may not be worth it, but a free listing is certainly a good ROI.
http://www.manta.com/

BUILD LINKS

ASK FOR "EASY" LINKS FROM ECOSYSTEM PARTNERS.

PROMOTE YOUR COMPANY!

- Inbound links matter for SEO.
- Ecosystem partners are customers, suppliers, trade show partners, etc.
- Many provide easy link opportunities.

DESCRIPTION: : Link building is a constant effort for effective SEO. Many companies struggle with link building. "Who would link to us?" they ask. The first easy link targets are your ecosystem partners. These are your customers, suppliers, affiliated businesses, trade shows, chambers of commerce -- businesses or organizations with whom you have a complementary, and not competitive, relationship. If you are a member of the local chamber of commerce, be sure to get a backlink from their website to yours. If you have many suppliers, be sure to ask for a link from their website to yours as a valued customer. If you participate in any trade shows, make sure that the online show directory links to your website. "You don't ask, you don't get."

BEST FOR: All organizations.

DO THIS: As often as possible.

TIME TO COMPLETE: A few hours or less.

HOW IMPORTANT IS THIS IS TO YOUR BUSINESS?

HOW IMPORTANT IS THIS IS TO YOUR BUSINESS?

< Not Important – Neutral – Very Important >
☐　　　☐☐☐　　　☐

WHAT GRADE DO YOU GIVE YOUR COMPANY ON THIS TASK?

☐ **Not Relevant | Grade: < F –D – C – B – A >**

TO-DO'S

- Identify ecosystem partners such as trade associations, suppliers, and even customers.
- Create a systematic process of asking for links.
- Follow up, follow up, follow up!
- Make link building a part of all your marketing, including real-world relationships.

The person assigned to do this is: _____.

Deadline to complete: _____, 201_.

LANDING PAGES

CREATE EFFECTIVE LANDING PAGES THAT FOLLOW THE CEA MODEL.

CREATE STRONG SEO CONTENT!

- Landing pages, in terms of SEO, are pages that focus on a key search.
- Landing pages should get you to the top of a target Google search.
- Users need to move from a landing page to a registration or purchase.

DESCRIPTION: Landing pages are critical for SEO, but confusing. Google Analytics defines a landing page as the first page that someone touches on your website. For instance, if you get to the top of the Google search for "industrial fans for agriculture" with a page on "industrial fans for agriculture," then when a user clicks from Google to that page, that page is your "landing page." More conceptually, a landing page is a page you specifically design to target a keyword phrase. Be sure to SEO optimize your landing pages, and then make them "one click" from your home page. Finally, think in terms of the CEA model: Confirm the user search, Engage the user to get him or her excited, and get an Action from the user, such as a registration or sale.

BEST FOR: All organizations.

DO THIS: As needed.

TIME TO COMPLETE: Each time, a few hours or less.

HOW IMPORTANT IS THIS IS TO YOUR BUSINESS?

< **Not Important – Neutral – Very Important** >
☐   ☐☐☐   ☐

WHAT GRADE DO YOU GIVE YOUR COMPANY ON THIS TASK?

☐ **Not Relevant | Grade:** < F –D – C – B – A >

TO-DO'S

- Map targeted, focused keyword families to individual landing pages.
- Optimize each landing page for "on page" SEO with great TITLE tags, etc.
- Make sure that each landing page is "one click" from your home page.
- Don't forget the landing experience -- a landing page should lead to a registration or sale.
- Focus, focus, focus -- a good website has no more than seven landing pages.

The person assigned to do this is: _____.

Deadline to complete: _____, 201_.

INTERNET RESOURCES

Effective Landing Page Design
Tutorial post and YouTube video explaining the ins and outs of effective landing pages for Search Engine Optimization.
http://www.jm-seo.org/seo-tutorial/seo-landingpage.html

REAL WORLD PROMOTION

LEVERAGE REAL-WORLD INTERACTIONS TO ONLINE RELATIONSHIPS.

PROMOTE YOUR COMPANY!

- Many businesses have real-world opportunities, like in-store conversations.
- Other opportunities include stickers, placards, and note cards.
- Employee training and incentives can boost real-world to social media/SEO.

DESCRIPTION: The world is merging: real-world interactions, SEO, Google, and social media are all becoming intertwined. Don't forget that your real-world interaction with customers is a way to grow your SEO and social media presence. Example: Train your employees to ask happy customers to review your business on Google+ Local. Reviews, of course, help with local SEO. Even better, incentivize your employees by giving them a bonus each time your business reviews hit a milestone such as 10 reviews, 20 reviews, etc. You can also identify some of your best customers as potential bloggers. People who love you and your business might make great content writers, to blog about new products or trends and thereby get you authentic, cheap content for your blog. Brainstorm ways that real-world interactions can become long-term online relationships!

BEST FOR: All organizations.

DO THIS: As often as possible.

TIME TO COMPLETE: Each time, a few hours or less.

HOW IMPORTANT IS THIS IS TO YOUR BUSINESS?

< Not Important – Neutral – Very Important >
☐   ☐☐☐   ☐

WHAT GRADE DO YOU GIVE YOUR COMPANY ON THIS TASK?

☐ **Not Relevant | Grade: < F –D – C – B – A >**

TO-DO'S

- Your website and social media can build on one-time real-world interactions to become continuous relationships online.
- You don't ask, you don't get -- train your employees to proactively ask customers for reviews on Google+, follow you on Facebook, etc.
- Brainstorm ideas like contests and promotions that can incentivize people to follow you on Twitter or Google+.
- Identify your best customers and consider hiring them as inexpensive content bloggers.
- Set aside a specific time for you and your team to brainstorm ways to leverage real-world contact into online relationships.

The person assigned to do this is: _____.

Deadline to complete: _____, 201_.

LINK METRICS

MEASURE YOUR PAGERANK VIA GOOGLE AND SURROGATE METRIC SERVICES.

MEASURE OR MONITOR YOUR PERFORMANCE!

- PageRank is a measure of your authority on the Web.
- Google does not share PageRank data in any detail, but surrogate measures exist.
- Use PageRank surrogate indicators as a metric in your SEO measurement strategy.

DESCRIPTION: PageRank, named after Google founder Larry Page, is simply a measurement of your website's authority on the Web. Think of the Web as high school, with the most popular kids at the top of the pecking order (New York Times, CNN, Oprah Winfrey), some in the middle, and some at the bottom or unknown. PageRank measures where your website is in this pecking order, giving you a score. Inbound links are the primary factor that influence PageRank. In addition, each URL on your site, as well as your domain, has a PageRank. The higher your PageRank, the more likely you are to score higher on a target search on Google. Google keeps much information on PageRank secret. As you build links, your PageRank improves, and you want to measure this improvement over time. Use surrogate services such as Opensiteexplorer.com to measure your PageRank over time as you work to climb the SEO pecking order!

BEST FOR: All organizations.

DO THIS: Monthly.

TIME TO COMPLETE: A few hours or less.

HOW IMPORTANT IS THIS IS TO YOUR BUSINESS?

< Not Important – Neutral – Very Important >
☐   ☐☐☐   ☐

WHAT GRADE DO YOU GIVE YOUR COMPANY ON THIS TASK?

☐ Not Relevant | Grade: < F – D – C – B – A >

TO-DO'S

- Measure your PageRank using a surrogate such as Opensiteexplorer.com.
- Engage in systematic link building as part of your SEO.
- Re-measure your inbound links and PageRank over time, looking for improvement.
- Compare your site to competitors using PageRank.
- Brainstorm new link building strategies to outcompete your competitors.

The person assigned to do this is: _____.

Deadline to complete: _____, 201_.

INTERNET RESOURCES

PRChecker -- PageRank Checker

You can check PageRank with the Google toolbar, but you can also check it with PRChecker. PageRank is Google's opinion of how popular you are -- how much authority your website has. Use it also to chart and target sites that might link to you and whether they are worth pursuing in a link strategy.
http://prchecker.info/

Open Site Explorer

Worried about the demise of the Yahoo site explorer? This new tool hopes to occupy that niche if or when Yahoo pulls the plug. Enter a URL and the tool will then identify the backlinks to that URL. Similar to Yahoo's site explorer and linkdiagnosis.com. A great new addition to the fleet of link analysis tools.
http://www.opensiteexplorer.org/

LinkDiagnosis

This fantastic free tool can show you all the important information about your competitors' links. The report includes PageRank, anchor texts, no-follow information and more. You enter your website, wait (a long time) as it meticulously goes through link after link, and ultimately gives you a nice report about backlinks to your website (or better yet, that of a competitor). Only installs on Firefox.
http://www.linkdiagnosis.com/

Majestic SEO

This company provides some pretty good link-checking tools. Nothing that you really can't get from other sites in an easier-to-use format. But still, if you are really researching who links to whom (comparing yourself vs. competitors), this tool is free and worth a look.
https://www.majesticseo.com/

SITEMAP

CREATE SOCIAL MEDIA CHANNELS AND BACKLINK TO YOUR WEBSITE.

CREATE STRONG SEO CONTENT!

- Google rewards sites that are SEO-friendly, and that includes sitemaps.
- An HTML sitemap helps both Google and human visitors navigate your website.
- An XML sitemap is an advanced technique for being Google-friendly.

DESCRIPTION: When you enter the Metropolitan Museum of Art in New York City, they provide a map of the museum. Is it necessary? Not exactly. It it helpful? Absolutely. A good map makes the museum easier to understand and easier to navigate. For websites, two types of sitemaps are needed. Fortunately, free tools make sitemaps easy. First, an HTML sitemap -- this usually exists as a link at the bottom of all pages, and helps Google (and humans) quickly see the navigational structure of your website. Second, an XML sitemap is a sitemap written in XML. You can submit this via Webmaster tools, and it tends to help Google find new HTML and image content on your site.

BEST FOR: All organizations.

DO THIS: One time.

TIME TO COMPLETE: A few hours or less.

HOW IMPORTANT IS THIS IS TO YOUR BUSINESS?

< Not Important – Neutral – Very Important >

☐   ☐☐☐   ☐

WHAT GRADE DO YOU GIVE YOUR COMPANY ON THIS TASK?

☐ **Not Relevant | Grade: < F –D – C – B – A >**

TO-DO'S

- Plan out your site architecture, if you have not already done so.
- Create an HTML sitemap and link from all pages, including your home page (usually in the footer).
- Use a free tool to create an XML sitemap.
- Upload the XML sitemap to your website.
- Alert Google and Bing to your sitemap via Webmaster Tools. Use robots.txt to reference your sitemap.

The person assigned to do this is: _____.

Deadline to complete: _____, 201_.

INTERNET RESOURCES

XML Sitemaps

This nifty free tool will make both an HTML and an XML map for your website. First, get your site properly organized. Second, use the tool to generate your HTML sitemap. Upload and link to that map. Third, use the tool to generate your XML sitemap. Upload that site to your root directory (e.g., http://www.jm-seo.org/sitemap.xml). Fourth, login to Google Webmaster tools and tell Google the location of your XML sitemap. You'll need to repeat this process when you do major updates to your site.
http://www.xml-sitemaps.com/

Google Webmaster Tools

Google's free Webmaster Tools allows you to communicate with Google about your site, including XML sitemaps. Sign up for this free service and then upload your XML sitemap.
https://www.google.com/webmasters/tools/home?hl=en

REVERSE ENGINEER LINKS

USE FREE TOOLS TO REVERSE ENGINEER COMPETITORS' LINK STRATEGIES.

CREATE STRONG SEO CONTENT!

- Google loves links and rewards highly linked sites in SEO.
- Reverse engineering your competitors' links can give you great ideas.
- Free tools make this easier than ever.

DESCRIPTION: Google loves links! (You can't say that enough.) But how do you get links? Ideas are the first step towards an effective link building strategy. How do you get ideas? One great way is to reverse engineer your competitors' link building strategies! The first step is to plug your competitors' website into one of the tools. The second step is to conceptualize the types of links that they have -- for instance, links from suppliers, links from non-profits, or even "link bait" links. The third step is to take those link targets and reverse engineer your own strategy to create similar (or better) links. SEO is a competitive sport, and link tools help you understand why other websites are outperforming you.

BEST FOR: All organizations.

DO THIS: Monthly.

TIME TO COMPLETE: Each time, a few hours or less.

HOW IMPORTANT IS THIS IS TO YOUR BUSINESS?

< Not Important – Neutral – Very Important >
☐   ☐☐☐   ☐

WHAT GRADE DO YOU GIVE YOUR COMPANY ON THIS TASK?

☐ **Not Relevant | Grade: < F –D – C – B – A >**

TO-DO'S

- Identify your SEO competitors, sites that are outperforming you on your target keywords.
- Plug a competitor's URL into one of the free link tools.
- Analyze the data that comes back, looking for individual links sites and link patterns.
- Reach out to the complementary sites identified that might also link to you.
- Conceptualize their link strategies and plug what you like into your own link strategy.

The person assigned to do this is: _____.

Deadline to complete: _____, 201_.

INTERNET RESOURCES

Open Site Explorer
Worried about the demise of the Yahoo site explorer? This new tool hopes to occupy that niche if or when Yahoo pulls the plug. Enter a URL and the tool will then identify the backlinks to that URL. Similar to Yahoo's site explorer and linkdiagnosis.com. A great new addition to the fleet of link analysis tools.
http://www.opensiteexplorer.org/

LinkDiagnosis
This fantastic free tool can show you all the important information about your competitors' links. The report includes PageRank, anchor texts, no-follow information and more. You enter your website, wait (a long time) as it meticulously goes thru link after link and ultimately gives you a nice report about backlinks to your website (or better yet, that of your competitor). Only installs on Firefox.
http://www.linkdiagnosis.com/

Majestic SEO
This company provides some pretty good link checking tools. Nothing that you really can't get from other sites, in an easier-to-use format. But still, if you are really researching who links to whom (comparing yourself vs. competitors), this tool is free and worth a look.
https://www.majesticseo.com/

Topsy
Real-time search engine of Twitter. You can also search the Web and Videos. VERY important: You can use this to input a URL -- say, jm-seo.org or chipestimate.com -- and see how frequently that URL and its sub URLs have been tweeted. A great way to see your social shares!
http://topsy.com/

TITLE TAG AUDIT

AUDIT YOUR TITLE TAGS FOR SEO KEYWORDS.

CREATE STRONG SEO CONTENT!

- The TITLE tag is the most powerful SEO tag on any page.
- Your home page TITLE tag is your most powerful website phrase.
- A TITLE tag audit double-checks if you are communicating with Google.

DESCRIPTION: In poll after poll, most SEO experts agree that having the target keyword/key phrase in the TITLE tag of an individual page is the most important "on page" factor as to whether a page shows up on a Google search. (Inbound links, of cours, matter a lot as well.) The TITLE tag controls 1) the phrase seen at the top of the browser, 2) the headline on a Google search, and 3) whether a page has a good chance of getting to the top of Google. A TITLE tag audit means going through all the TITLE tags of your website and making sure that they are unique, accurate (reflect real keyword content on the page), and fit within the 69 characters displayed by Google. (You can go as long as 80 characters, with the understanding that Google stops indexing somewhere around 80 characters.)

BEST FOR: All organizations.

DO THIS: One time.

TIME TO COMPLETE: More than a few hours.

HOW IMPORTANT IS THIS IS TO YOUR BUSINESS?

< Not Important – Neutral – Very Important >
☐   ☐☐☐   ☐

WHAT GRADE DO YOU GIVE YOUR COMPANY ON THIS TASK?

☐ **Not Relevant | Grade: < F –D – C – B – A >**

TO-DO'S

- Set aside time for a TITLE tag audit of your website content vs. SEO.
- Identify and prioritize your target keywords.
- Put your most important, strategic keywords in your home page TITLE tag.
- On every other page, make sure that the TITLE tag contains the target keywords.
- Make sure each TITLE tag is unique and accurate.

The person assigned to do this is: _____.

Deadline to complete: _____, 201_.

INTERNET RESOURCES

TITLE Tag Relevancy Checker

This tool will evaluate how your existing TITLE Tag relates to the content that is on your page, and it can suggest an order for the words based upon your content. The Title Creator Tool can also evaluate a new webpage title for you to compare to your existing title. http://int-seo.com/title_creator_tool.php

SEO Page Tag Counter Tool

The TITLE tag should be less than 69 visible characters. The META DESCRIPTION should be less than 155 characters. This free tool allows you to input your text and count it automatically. Great for using as you write these two important META TAGS for SEO. http://intinc.com/support/title-description-tag-free-counter-tool.htm

META DESCRIPTION TAG AUDIT

AUDIT YOUR META DESCRIPTION TAGS FOR SEO KEYWORDS.

CREATE STRONG SEO CONTENT!

- The META DESCRIPTION tag heavily influences your page summaries on Google.
- A good META DESCRIPTION tag contains the target keywords yet is also exciting.
- A META DESCRIPTION tag audit double-checks if you are communicating with Google.

DESCRIPTION: Think of your META DESCRIPTION tag as your suggestion to Google for how to describe your home page and every other page on your website. The character limit is 155 characters. Be sure to include your target keywords in the META DESCRIPTION tag and also add pithy, exciting phrases that will "get the click." The purpose of the META DESCRIPTION tag is not only to accurately describe page keyword content but to persuade the user to click over from Google.

BEST FOR: All organizations.

DO THIS: One time.

TIME TO COMPLETE: More than a few hours.

HOW IMPORTANT IS THIS IS TO YOUR BUSINESS?

> **< Not Important – Neutral – Very Important >**
> ☐   ☐☐☐   ☐

WHAT GRADE DO YOU GIVE YOUR COMPANY ON THIS TASK?

☐ **Not Relevant | Grade: < F –D – C – B – A >**

TO-DO'S

- Set aside time for a META DESCRIPTION tag audit of your website content vs. SEO.
- Identify and prioritize your target keywords.
- Put your most important, strategic keywords in your home page META DESCRIPTION tag.
- For every individual webpage, ensure that its META DESCRIPTION tag contains the target keywords.
- Make sure each META DESCRIPTION tag is unique and accurate.

The person assigned to do this is: _____.

Deadline to complete: _____, 201_.

INTERNET RESOURCES

Letter Count Utility

The TITLE tag should be less than 80 characters, with the most important being the first 66 characters. Your META DESCRIPTION should be less than 155 characters. Use this nifty online tool to copy/paste your tag text and it will automatically count the characters and spaces for you.
http://www.lettercount.com/

Meta Tag Analyzer from SEOCentro

SeoCentro designed this Meta Tag analysis tool to help webmasters analyze their web pages. This tool not only analyzes the Meta Tags, but analyzes where your keywords are positioned, plus gives you information on keyword density. When using Firefox, use CTRL+F to highlight your keywords in the result. In doing so, you can quickly check to see if a target keyword is well positioned vis-a-vis important tags like the TITLE or META DESCRIPTION tag.
http://www.seocentro.com/tools/search-engines/metatag-analyzer.html

SEO Page Tag Counter Tool

The TITLE tag should be less than 69 visible characters. The META DESCRIPTION should be less than 155 characters. This free tool allows you to input your text and count it automatically. Great for using as you write these two important META TAGS for SEO.
http://intinc.com/support/title-description-tag-free-counter-tool.htm

META KEYWORDS TAG AUDIT

THE META KEYWORDS TAG DOES NOT MATTER.

CREATE STRONG SEO CONTENT!

- The META KEYWORDS tag is ignored by Google and Bing.
- Yet many people still use it.
- Worse still, it confuses people into thinking that they are "done" with SEO.

DESCRIPTION: Just when you thought SEO couldn't be more confusing, along comes the META KEYWORDS tag. This tag is officially ignored by both Google and Bing, yet still exists in many platforms such as WordPress, GoDaddy's WebSite Tonight, Teamsite, and many other common CMS (Content Management Systems). The tragedy is that your staff may be entering their content, inputting keywords into the META KEYWORD tag and thinking that they have "done" their SEO. They then ignore the tags that really do matter -- such as the TITLE tag, META description tag, header tags, IMG ALT tags, etc. So educate your staff that the META KEYWORD tag does not matter, and they should instead focus on what actually does matter.

BEST FOR: All organizations.

DO THIS: One time.

TIME TO COMPLETE: A few hours or less.

HOW IMPORTANT IS THIS IS TO YOUR BUSINESS?

< Not Important – Neutral – Very Important >
☐   ☐☐☐   ☐

WHAT GRADE DO YOU GIVE YOUR COMPANY ON THIS TASK?

☐ Not Relevant | Grade: < F –D – C – B – A >

TO-DO'S

- Alert your staff that the META KEYWORDS tag has zero impact.
- Clarify the difference between the META KEYWORDS tag and tags that actually do matter.
- Don't confuse the META KEYWORDS tag with other META tags like the DESCRIPTION tag.
- Don't confuse the META KEYWORDS tag with blog tagging, as in WordPress.

The person assigned to do this is: _____.

Deadline to complete: _____, 201_.

INTERNET RESOURCES

Google Ignores the META KEYWORDS tag

Here is the official announcement by Google that, yes, they ignore the META KEYWORD tag.

http://googlewebmastercentral.blogspot.com/2009/09/google-does-not-use-keywords-meta-tag.html

SEO CONTENT

WRITE KEYWORD-HEAVY, WELL-STRUCTURED, SEO-FRIENDLY CONTENT.

CREATE STRONG SEO CONTENT!

- Content is king, especially content that uses HTML tags correctly.
- Keyword-heavy content is critically important to SEO, so know your keywords.
- Google prefers text-heavy pages.

DESCRIPTION: No phrase is more common on the Web for SEO than the phrase "content is king." Once you know your SEO keyword targets, inventory your existing pages on your website to check that they have good keyword density for your SEO targets. But keyword density is more than just the percentage of keywords on the page. It is also weaving the keywords into "natural syntax" of subject, verb, object, as Google rewards pages with not only good keyword density but effective natural syntax. Writing SEO-friendly content should become a process informing your blog, your new product pages, your press releases and all content on your website down to the titles, descriptions, and even comments posted to your YouTube videos. Content is king!

BEST FOR: All businesses.

DO THIS: As often as possible.

TIME TO COMPLETE: An hour or less.

HOW IMPORTANT IS THIS IS TO YOUR BUSINESS?

< Not Important – Neutral – Very Important >
☐   ☐☐☐   ☐

WHAT GRADE DO YOU GIVE YOUR COMPANY ON THIS TASK?

☐ Not Relevant | Grade: < F –D – C – B – A >

TO-DO'S

- Identify your target SEO keywords.
- Inventory your existing content vs. your target keywords.
- Check your page keyword density, including tag structure.
- Create an ongoing process of rolling out new keyword-heavy content.

The person assigned to do this is: _____.

Deadline to complete: _____, 201_.

INTERNET RESOURCES

Google Keyword Tool
To write great SEO-friendly content, you must know your keywords. Use this free Google tool to identify high-volume, high-value keywords, plus helper words that make a single keyword into a multiple keyowrd phrase. Knowing good keywords is a must for writing good SEO content!
https://adwords.google.com/select/KeywordToolExternal

Keyword Density Calculator
This simple but nifty tool will take a website (your website, a competitor's website, any page that interests you on the Web) and analyze it for one-, two-, and three-word keyword density. It's great for both reverse engineering a competitor and/or double-checking your own SEO work.
http://www.xml-sitemaps.com/keyword-density-tool.html

Metamend -- Keyword Density Tool
Pop a URL from your own site, or that of a competitor, into this tool. Look at the tag cloud that is created for keyword ideas and a keyword checkup.
http://www.metamend.com/seo-tools/keyword-density-analyzer.html

SPEED CHECK

CHECK YOUR WEBSITE'S SPEED IN GOOGLE WEBMASTER TOOLS.

MEASURE OR MONITOR YOUR PERFORMANCE!

- Google rewards speedy websites.
- Use free tools to monitor your website.
- Make a speed check a monthly ritual for your website SEO.

DESCRIPTION: One of the metrics that Google pays more and more attention to is your website response speed. Your website might be fast, or slow, or perhaps you don't even know. Fortunately, free tools exist to measure your website response speed and even give you (or your web developer) tips on how to improve your website speed. In addition, you can compare your site to others and consider changing ISPs, or perhaps complaining to them to get you on a faster service. Speed matters!

BEST FOR: All organizations.

DO THIS: Monthly.

TIME TO COMPLETE: An hour or less.

HOW IMPORTANT IS THIS IS TO YOUR BUSINESS?

< **Not Important – Neutral – Very Important** >
☐   ☐☐☐   ☐

WHAT GRADE DO YOU GIVE YOUR COMPANY ON THIS TASK?

☐ **Not Relevant | Grade: < F –D – C – B – A >**

TO-DO'S

- Go to one of the free speed tools.
- Measure your website speed. If you are slower than 20% of websites, be concerned.
- Get recommendations on how to improve speed.
- Have your web developer fix your site.

The person assigned to do this is: _____.

Deadline to complete: _____, 201_.

INTERNET RESOURCES

Google's Free Page Speed Tool

This is a new, amazing free tool from Google! Find out how fast they find your site to be, and get suggestions on how to improve its speed. Google penalizes sites that are slow. If your website is slower than 70% of sites on the Internet, you have reason to be concerned that it may be too slow to show up in Google searches.
https://developers.google.com/pagespeed/

Pingdom Tools

Offers diagnostic tools to find out key measurements, such as how fast your website loads. Useful for optimizing your website performance, which is increasingly important to Google.
http://tools.pingdom.com/

Google Webmaster Tools

Pop a URL from your own site, or that of a competitor, into this tool. Look at the tag cloud that is created for keyword ideas and a keyword checkup.
http://www.google.com/webmasters/tools

GOOGLE+ COMPANY PAGE

SET UP A GOOGLE+ COMPANY PAGE AND START GOOGLE+'ING.

PROMOTE YOUR COMPANY!

- Google+ is Google's new social network, heavily favored by Google.

- Setting up a company page on Google+ is easy to do.

- If Google+ takes off, you will be ready! If not, you haven't invested much.

DESCRIPTION: Google+ is Google's answer to Facebook, and Google+ pages for business parallel Facebook business pages. So the good news is if you already have a Facebook page for your business, Google+ isn't that difficult. The main difference is in audience. The Google+ audience tends to be more serious, more techie, and more male, so proceed accordingly. Another main difference is that Google+ authorship (i.e., rich snippets, get your picture to show on Google searches) works ONLY for personal pages, so I recommend you set up a Google+ personal page as well for a company spokesperson like your CEO or CTO. Finally, don't forget to use the Google+ badge to promote your Google+ company page.

BEST FOR: All organizations.

DO THIS: One time.

TIME TO COMPLETE: Each time, a few hours or less.

HOW IMPORTANT IS THIS IS TO YOUR BUSINESS?

< **Not Important – Neutral – Very Important** >
☐   ☐☐☐   ☐

WHAT GRADE DO YOU GIVE YOUR COMPANY ON THIS TASK?

☐ **Not Relevant | Grade:** < F –D – C – B – A >

TO-DO'S

- Sign up for Google+ at both a personal and corporate level.
- Don't confuse Google+ personal pages with authorship or with Google+ business pages.
- Conceptualize a strong Google+ corporate strategy for posting and engagement with users.
- Promote your Google+ business page with a Google+ badge.
- Remember, Google+ is still in its infancy.

The person assigned to do this is: _____.

Deadline to complete: _____, 201_.

INTERNET RESOURCES

Google+ for Business

Google+ is a competitive network to Facebook, and this is the official page to learn about putting your business on Google+. This page is the "go to" page for Google+, so start here as you learn how to put your business on Google+.
http://www.google.com/+/business/

Google+ For Business (+1 Button and Google+ Badge)

Here is Google's official gateway page to both the +1 button and the Google+ Badge. Get the code for either (or both) and add to your website.
http://www.google.com/+/business/promote.html

IDENTIFY BLOGGERS

FIND BLOGGERS WHO WANT TO BLOG ABOUT YOUR PRODUCTS OR SERVICES.

PROMOTE YOUR COMPANY!

- Generating SEO buzz starts with identifying the buzzers.
- Google Blog Search is the easiest way to find relevant bloggers.
- Brainstorm reasons why they'd want to blog about your company.

DESCRIPTION: When you say blog, most people think that they need to be writing the blog content. That's often true, and that's an important tactic in the blogosphere. However, a second tactic for effective blogging is to identify bloggers who are interested in your company's products or services. Google Blog Search should be your first stop. But beyond that, you have to brainstorm why bloggers might care about your news release, your new product announcement, or whatever you have that's new and exciting in your industry. Selling a blogger is like selling an editor: think of what's in it for them and their readers.

BEST FOR: All organizations.

DO THIS: As often as possible.

TIME TO COMPLETE: More than a few hours.

HOW IMPORTANT IS THIS IS TO YOUR BUSINESS?

< Not Important – Neutral – Very Important >
☐ ☐☐☐ ☐

WHAT GRADE DO YOU GIVE YOUR COMPANY ON THIS TASK?

☐ **Not Relevant | Grade: < F –D – C – B – A >**

TO-DO'S

- Know your important SEO keywords.
- Use Google Blog Search to identify bloggers who might cover your topics.
- Brainstorm reasons why each blogger might care enough to write about you.
- Reach out to bloggers, one by one, in a personalized way.
- Build a long-term contact list of bloggers.

The person assigned to do this is: _____.

Deadline to complete: _____, 201_.

INTERNET RESOURCES

Google Blog Search

Google Blog Search is an amazing and easy way to identify bloggers who care about your keywords. Simply type your keyword into Google and then on the left side. On the results page, click on "More." Then click on "Blogs." Or, use the URL provided here, and go directly to Google blog search. After you've searched for your keyword, on the left side of the results page, you can then sort by recency (past month, past week, etc.).
http://www.google.com/blogsearch

IceRocket

IceRocket is a competitor to Google blog search. Just enter your target SEO keywords and identify people who have blogged on that topic.
http://www.icerocket.com/

Google Alerts

According to Google, Google Alerts are email updates of the latest relevant Google results (web, news, etc.) based on your queries. Enter a search query you wish to monitor. You will see a preview of the type of results you'll receive. You could choose to receive results for a) your company name, b) your target keywords, and/or c) your competitors' names, and then Google will alert you to things it finds such as blog posts, news stories, or web pages on those topics. For blogs, use the pull-down to select just blogs for alerts on the blogosphere.
http://www.google.com/alerts

WEBSITE GOALS

IDENTIFY GOALS FOR YOUR WEBSITE.

DEFINE YOUR DESIRED ACTIONS!

- Defining your marketing goals will help you define subordinate SEO goals.
- Good Google rank, registrations, and/or purchases are common goals.
- Use Google Analytics to measure goal performance over time.

DESCRIPTION: Remember when they used to ask you, "What do you want to be when you grow up?" Well, now you've grown up. Take a look at your website, and ask it what it wants to be when it grows up. What are the goals of your website? Commonly, companies want their site to be a place where individuals will register for something free (a free demo, a free consult, etc.), and thereby become a sales lead and a captured email address for further marketing. Other companies are e-commerce oriented, so they seek to get actual sales on their website. From a broader marketing perspective, many companies have goals such as getting to the top of Google (Google rank), getting strong branding, and even growing recommendations and referrals (social media). Define your business goals and then drill down to Google Analytics for more.

BEST FOR: All organizations.

DO THIS: As needed.

TIME TO COMPLETE: More than a few hours.

HOW IMPORTANT IS THIS IS TO YOUR BUSINESS?

< Not Important – Neutral – Very Important >
☐   ☐☐☐   ☐

WHAT GRADE DO YOU GIVE YOUR COMPANY ON THIS TASK?

☐ **Not Relevant | Grade: < F –D – C – B – A >**

TO-DO'S

- Know your important SEO keywords.
- Use Google Blog Search to identify bloggers who might cover your topics.
- Brainstorm reasons why each blogger might care enough to write about you.
- Reach out to bloggers, one by one, in a personalized way.
- Build a long-term contact list of bloggers.

The person assigned to do this is: _____.

Deadline to complete: _____, 201_.

INTERNET RESOURCES

SEOBook -- Firefox Rank Checker

Sign up for a free account, and you can use this tool to track your rank on Google. It works only on Firefox, so be sure to install Firefox first. Then, follow these steps. First, input your domain; be sure to use lowercase. Second, input your keyword list. Third, input any competitor names. This handy tool will track your SERP rank (your position on a Google search). Ultimately, you need to be at least in the top ten.
http://www.seobook.com/

Google Analytics

Google Analytics is the enterprise-class web analytics solution that gives you rich insights into your website traffic and marketing effectiveness. Powerful, flexible and easy-to-use features now let you see and analyze your traffic data in an entirely new way. With Google Analytics, you're more prepared to write better-targeted ads, strengthen your marketing initiatives and create higher converting websites.
http://www.google.com/analytics/

Goals in Google Analytics (Free Video)

Goals are incredibly important to Web metrics. Watch this informative free video from Google on goals in Analytics. Then circle back to your website and define your goals. Use Advanced Segments to define whether your goals are being achieved over a given time period.
http://services.google.com/analytics/breeze/en/v5/goals_v20_ad1/

Google Analytics Goals Explained

Here is the (overly) informative article from Google on what conversions and goals are in Analytics. Feed this information back into your metrics, goals, and Google Analytics strategy.
https://support.google.com/analytics/bin/answer.py?hl=en&answer=1006230&topic=16 31741&rd=1

REFERRALS IN GOOGLE ANALYTICS

DISCOVER AND NURTURE REFERRAL WEBSITES.

MEASURE OR MONITOR YOUR PERFORMANCE!

- Discover who your friends are (i.e, friends on the Web).
- Referrer websites are blogs, portals, etc., that send you traffic.
- You can also measure social media performance to your website.

DESCRIPTION: In Google Analytics, referral website are websites that "refer" traffic to you. If, for instance, you have a strong YouTube channel and strong YouTube videos with links from YouTube to your website, then you can use referral information to measure how many visits you get from YouTube. Other referrals might come from blogs, publications and partner websites that link to you. Combined with Google Analytics, referral information can measure how many goals (e.g., registration or purchases) are completed by people coming from a referral website. You can thus verify who your friends are on the Web (or how well non-Google advertising platforms like Facebook ads are performing), as well as discover new sites that actively refer traffic to you and build on that relationship.

BEST FOR: All organizations.

DO THIS: Monthly.

TIME TO COMPLETE: A few hours or less.

HOW IMPORTANT IS THIS IS TO YOUR BUSINESS?

< **Not Important – Neutral – Very Important** >
☐ ☐☐☐ ☐

WHAT GRADE DO YOU GIVE YOUR COMPANY ON THIS TASK?

☐ **Not Relevant | Grade: < F –D – C – B – A >**

TO-DO'S

- Set up Google Analytics.
- In Google Analytics, click on Traffic Sources, Sources, Referrals on the left.
- If desired, set up a custom Advanced Segment to view referrers from a particular site.
- In addition, use "goals" in Advanced Segments to measure goal performance vs. target referral sites.
- Look for referrals who refer a few visits, to grow a relationship and grow more traffic.

The person assigned to do this is: _____.

Deadline to complete: _____, 201_.

INTERNET RESOURCES

Google Analytics

Google Analytics is the enterprise-class web analytics solution that gives you rich insights into your website traffic and marketing effectiveness. Powerful, flexible and easy-to-use features now let you see and analyze your traffic data in an entirely new way. With Google Analytics, you're more prepared to write better-targeted ads, strengthen your marketing initiatives and create higher converting websites.
http://www.google.com/analytics/

Referral Traffic in Google Analytics

Here is the official help file from Google on referrals. If you're trying to build a traffic stream from referrals, you want to know which domains are successful sources. For example, if you're posting videos on YouTube in order to raise brand awareness, you want to see whether those videos are driving visitors to your site, and consequently whether youtube.com shows up as a top source of referrals.
http://support.google.com/analytics/bin/answer.py?hl=en&answer=1247839

ADVANCED SEGMENTS

USE ADVANCED SEGMENTS TO EXPLORE CUSTOMER GROUPS.

MEASURE OR MONITOR YOUR PERFORMANCE!

- Slice and dice who comes to your website, and from where.
- Understand not just the raw traffic numbers, but what they do on your site.
- Drill down into data such as keywords, referrers, and goals.

DESCRIPTION: Google Analytics is a powerful free platform for understanding how prospects get to your website and what they do on your site once they land. Advanced Segments and custom Advanced Segments allow you to segment your web traffic by practically any variable. For example, if you would like to know what percent of your traffic comes from organic (free) SEO traffic vs. what percent comes from paid advertising, Advanced Segments can tell you that. Or if you'd like to know how many people complete a defined goal on your site (e.g., a purchase or a registration), custom Advanced Segments can tell you that, even down to the slicing and dicing of whether SEO leads are more likely to complete your goal than AdWords leads. You can even segment by referrers (e.g., press release traffic), or geographics (like Texas vs. New York).

BEST FOR: All organizations.

DO THIS: One time.

TIME TO COMPLETE: An hour or less.

HOW IMPORTANT IS THIS IS TO YOUR BUSINESS?

< Not Important – Neutral – Very Important >
☐ ☐☐☐ ☐

WHAT GRADE DO YOU GIVE YOUR COMPANY ON THIS TASK?

☐ **Not Relevant | Grade: < F –D – C – B – A >**

TO-DO'S

- Define a marketing question you want answered, such as Texas customers vs. NY customers.
- Login to Google Analytics, click on Advanced Segments, and new custom segment.
- Select your parameters in the menus provided, such as medium = organic for organic, SEO traffic.
- Don't forget to use the Google Analytics "help" function if you do not understand the vocabulary!
- Save your Advanced Segment and use it as a window into a specific segment of your web traffic.

The person assigned to do this is: _____.

Deadline to complete: _____, 201_.

INTERNET RESOURCES

Google Analytics IQ Lessons

If you are using Google Analytics, this is a must-see treasure trove of information on how to use that powerful platform. Ironically, it can be very difficult to jump from Google Analytics over to the Google IQ Lessons site. Only Google knows why they made it so difficult. That said, check out the topics and videos here. If you are reallys serious you can study and get qualified as an Analytics Expert!

http://www.google.com/intl/en/analytics/iq.html?